MW00425352

FAITH
&
REASON

HENRI BLOCHER

FAITH
&
REASON

HENDRICKSON
PUBLISHERS

Faith and Reason

© 2017 Hendrickson Publishers Marketing, LLC
P. O. Box 3473
Peabody, Massachusetts 01961-3473
www.hendrickson.com

ISBN 978-1-61970-957-7

All rights reserved. No part of this book may be reproduced or transmitted in any form or by any means, electronic or mechanical, including photocopying, recording, or by any information storage and retrieval system, without permission in writing from the publisher.

Scripture quotations marked (NIV) are taken from the Holy Bible, New International Version˙, NIV˙. Copyright © 1973, 1978, 1984, 2011 by Biblica, Inc.™ Used by permission of Zondervan. All rights reserved worldwide. www.zondervan .com. The "NIV" and "New International Version" are trademarks registered in the United States Patent and Trademark Office by Biblica, Inc.™

Scripture quotations marked (ESV) are taken from the Holy Bible, English Standard Version (ESV®), copyright © 2001, by Crossway, a publishing ministry of Good News Publishers. Used by permission. All rights reserved.

Scripture quotations marked RSV are taken from the Revised Standard Version of the Bible, copyright © 1946, 1952, 1971 by the Division of Christian Education of the National Council of the Churches of Christ in the United States of America. Used by permission. All rights reserved.

Scripture quotations marked NKJV are taken from the New King James Version®. Copyright © 1982 by Thomas Nelson. Used by permission. All rights reserved.

Scripture quotations marked (TLB) are taken from The Living Bible copyright © 1971. Used by permission of Tyndale House Publishers, Inc., Carol Stream, Illinois 60188. All rights reserved.

Scripture quotations not marked are the author's translation.

Printed in the United States of America

First Printing—August 2017

Library of Congress Cataloging-in-Publication Data

Names: Blocher, Henri, author. | DiMauro, Damon, translator.
Title: Faith and reason / Henri Blocher ; translated by Damon DiMauro.
Other titles: La foi et la raison. English
Description: Peabody, Massachusetts : Hendrickson Publishers, [2017] |
    Includes bibliographical references.
Identifiers: LCCN 2017014136 | ISBN 9781619709577 (alk. paper)
Subjects: LCSH: Faith and reason--Christianity. | Apologetics.
Classification: LCC BT50 .B5413 2017 | DDC 231/.042--dc23
    LC record available at https://lccn.loc.gov/2017014136

CONTENTS

Introduction: From Youthful Memory to Everyone's Mission   1

1. The Recourse to Reason in the Affirmation of the Faith   7

     Historical Survey   7
     Evangelicals and Apologetics   9
     The French Scene   11
     The Fundamental Question   13

2. Rationalism in the Light of Scripture   23

     Rationalism   24
     The Observations of Experience   24
     Biblical Teaching   28
     On What Basis Can There Be Dialogue?   31
     How Long to Persevere?   33

3. Reflection on an Objection to the Faith: "You can make the Bible say whatever you want"   35

     The Transmission of the Biblical Text   38
     The Successive Editions/Versions of the Text?   41
     The Bible, a Contradictory Book?   43

4. Response to the Objection: "Scientific endeavor is contrary to faith"   57

     Modern Science   58
     Miscellaneous Objections   60
     Objections on the Basis of Principles   60

5. Response to the Objection: "The findings of scientific
   research show the Bible to be in error, and most
   especially when it comes to miracles"   77

      Minor Errors Here and There?   78
      The Structure of Reality   80
      Science and Faith in Relation to Origins   85
      The Question of Miracles   91
      The Objection to Miracles   93
      The Case for Miracles   95
      Conclusion   104

Conclusion   105

For Further Reading: A Short Select Bibliography   107

About the Author / Translator   111

INTRODUCTION

FROM YOUTHFUL MEMORY
TO EVERYONE'S MISSION

The memory has remained etched in my mind. It takes me back to a bygone era (I have nothing to hide!) when I was thirteen or fourteen years old. The attempt to argue on behalf of the gospel was not well regarded in the circles around me, and my coming-of-age sensibilities had been instilled with the prevailing negative attitude (yet I was already interested in such things). Along comes a pastor-theologian from Athens, Greece, on a visit to the evangelical communities of the Paris region. I recall his name: Metallinos. His ministry was bearing great fruit: a growing church, the founding of a Bible institute, etc. I thus listen to him with respectful attention. I hear him highlight the role that his expositions on *apologetics* play for him in the furtherance of the Cause. I am stunned. The impact of the shock will no doubt later help me understand that a negative attitude toward apologetics is not in fact justified by biblical teaching—that in order to overcome an ill-conceived apologetics, for this kind has indeed existed, we need a *well-conceived* apologetics.

The term "apologetics" comes from Greek, and derives directly from a word the New Testament employs several times. Apologetics is the art and science of *apologia*, whose meaning is somewhat broader than that of our own "apology" (Fr. *faire l'apologie de*, to excuse, rationalize). What is an *apologia*? It is a defense, in the first instance before a tribunal. The meaning then extends to apply to an ordered, reasonable, and reasoned discourse, seeking to justify a position—or a person—so as to defend against an accusation, with a view to bringing about a favorable outcome. The prefix *apo* indicates a context of reply; *logia* is akin to *logos*, which implies reason, deliberation. The sum is that apologetics is about holding yourself accountable for the positions that you advocate. The apostle Paul can thus say that he has been appointed for the *"apologia"* of the gospel (Philippians 1:16), namely that he has adopted a discourse that persuades, if possible, his hearers and leads them to faith.

Another use of the term, in a verse which relates directly to the central point of our subject, is particularly interesting. It occurs in 1 Peter 3. The apostle, in context, is exhorting the faithful to patience and purity in conduct. Those whom he is addressing also find themselves in a situation of hostility; they are already persecuted: indeed, they have been cast into the "fiery ordeal" of testing (1 Peter 4:12 NIV). They should not be surprised by it, but rather consider themselves blessed to suffer for righteousness' sake. If they are mistreated because they have acted justly, it is an honor that the Lord bestows on them. "But in your hearts reverence Christ as Lord," the apostle tells them (1 Peter 3:15 RSV). Peter here borrows a phrase from the prophet Isaiah, which reads, "Give to the LORD (YHWH, Jehovah) the place due him, the place due the most holy God." He applies it to Christ identified as the Lord, in order to encourage the faithful not to shrink back from giving him all the honor due him, even at the very cost of their lives through persecution. "Always be prepared to make a defense [*apologia*] to any one who calls you to account for the hope that is in you, yet do it with gentleness and reverence; and keep your conscience clear, so that, when you are abused, those who revile your good behavior in Christ may be put to shame" (1 Peter 3:15–16 RSV; Peter employs here the same substantive which signifies, as I explained above, the type of discourse that a lawyer, a politician, or a philosopher might pronounce in support of his positions). Peter calls for an apology "against," or rather "directed toward," whoever requests a "reason," whoever requests "an account": With what arguments then do you justify your expectation? Why do you invest all your resources, indeed why do you lay down your very life, to follow this Jesus whom you call Christ? Christians must be ready, according to Peter's exhortation, to have a discourse prepared which defends the commitment they have made, to give a "reason" for the hope that is in them.

Such is the task of the apologist, and we will note here that it involves the exercise of "reason," as the word Peter employs in the original (*logos*) is normally translated ("account" is also possible). In the New Testament, we can see that the apostles, fully inspired by the Lord—they were not gaffe-prone when speaking in his name (though fallible in personal conduct, in apostolic teaching they were Spirit-led)—"did apologetics." They prepared discourses which made appeal, in certain respects, to arguments, and that for the purpose of leading their hearers to faith, or rather to confirm them in faith if they were already converted. The relationship between the exercise of reason and the commitment of faith remains an obscure enigma for many, believers and unbelievers alike, which is why the pages that follow treat this relationship first and foremost. They do not claim to treat the topic of apologetics in great depth. They leave aside many theoretical problems or conversely those more linked to practical concerns—notably *the* problem of problems, namely that of *evil*, which I have addressed in my book *Evil and the Cross*. Instead, this book takes as its focus of study the use of reason that has held sway over modernity, and decidedly over a large swath of our "late modernity." The use of reason in *science*, including the natural sciences, with its method of empirical experimentation and its recourse to mathematics, offers the model. The "science and faith" debate thus plays an important role here. However, the ambition of this sketch is to situate the various topics raised along the way within their wider worldview context, and the context of ultimate concerns relative to the purpose of life itself.

Right motivation matters. Do we engage in apologetics for the pure pleasure of the interplay of ideas (for the back and forth of argument can often resemble a ping-pong match)? Do we try to crush the "adversary" only to show off our own superiority? Or even do we aim only toward a utilitarian purpose, such as expanding church rolls by recruiting new members? I doubt that endeavors driven by such motives will bear much fruit for the kingdom, or that they will enjoy the favor of divine blessing.

There are three reasons for seeking out with perseverance the most persuasive reasons for believing (i.e., to engage in apologetics). Considerations which are carefully weighed, closely examined, based on the known facts and the coherence of cause and effect, render the decision for faith *responsible*. Such is their primary function. Certainly, God, in his free mercy, can suddenly awaken faith in an individual, without there being a rational conscious process on his part (though we can suppose unconscious preparations at work): God can touch, it seems, through just emotions. However, in general, he wishes to *raise* his sons and daughters, his covenant partners, to be responsible. He prefers that they become committed to faith in an intelligent and deliberative manner (like the Bereans in Acts 17:11; see 1 Corinthians 10:15 and 14:20). Otherwise, whom do they really believe and what do they really believe? Any manipulator is capable of moving emotions. Serious arguments make all the difference between faith and *credulity*. Biblical faith is the opposite of credulity.

The second function of apologetics is to put into practice *love* for our neighbor. Nothing less. If Christ's love draws us toward our neighbor, filling us with the desire to have him see at last the Truth of Grace, we will not want to manipulate him, which would only serve to diminish him. We will not be content to present him with the Act of Christ and the offer of Salvation matter-of-factly. We will try to persuade him, because, loving him in God's way, we desire his good. We will seek to enter into his thought processes and to suggest reasons which will shake him, reasons which will break down his mental strongholds and disabuse him of his fallacies (cf. 2 Corinthians 10:4–5). If we make no effort in this vein (adapted, adjusted, to each person), we hardly love him, and rather we love him amiss.

The third function should stimulate in us the strongest motivation: by seeking persuasive reasons for faith, we give *glory* to God. It is a matter of demonstrating that we love him with all our *mind*. We want to focus, as a lens does the rays of the sun, the brilliance of his *Name*—this splendor that all his works reflect (Psalm 8), this witness to his power and his divinity which the heavens and the earth proclaim (Psalm 19; Romans 1). By the same token, we want to erase the stain which unbelief represents, for he who does not receive the testimony of God makes God a liar (1 John 5:9–10). The philosopher Bertrand Russell used to claim that were he to be questioned by the Sovereign Judge at the Last Judgment (a doctrine which he derided, of course, as a myth), he would justify his refusal to believe in these terms: "Not enough evidence! Not enough evidence!" Now, therein lies an impudence which apologetics must combat! The God whose grace has taken hold of us is the God of Truth, who possesses in himself the principle of revelation, to wit his logos or Word: he wants to express and to reveal who he is in his magnificence—which is his glory. He has also created us in his image with the capacity to recognize him: our understanding of his revelation serves to mirror his glory. However weak and defective our minds may be, however dented and rusted the mirror, we begin to glorify God when we seek out the reasons in support of his existence.

Thus understood and contextualized, apologetics is part and parcel of the mission of the church. For those who enjoy punning, we might then speak here of her "Apolo Mission"!

The following chapters reproduce studies presented to the brothers and sisters of my church during the monthly meetings which we (somewhat pompously) referred to as the "biblical institute of the Tabernacle." From recordings made during these sessions, my pastor (and wonderful friend) Mr. Thierry Huser has established the text, for which I cannot thank him enough! He has provided the "substrate" of the revision that I have undertaken, with some additions, for the present publication.

I hope the reader, his curiosity whetted, will pursue his investigations further still, in availing himself, for example, of the works cited in the bibliography.

1

THE RECOURSE TO REASON IN THE AFFIRMATION OF THE FAITH

Historical Survey

The first-century Christians patterned themselves after the example of the apostles. Apologetics was considered an activity of vital importance. The first theologians, too, in the second century, were apologetes (or apologists). Those who applied themselves then to systematic reflection, that is, to presenting the Christian faith in an orderly manner, did so not as professors of theology for the equipping of future pastors, but as defenders of Christianity against accusations on the part of pagans. They acted as interpreters, or as "persuaders," with respect to those they addressed. We might cite here Justin Martyr, a philosopher before his conversion to Christianity, who rose to become the principal apologist of the second century, among those to whom we refer as the "apologete Fathers." The need for apologetics went unquestioned thereafter for hundreds of years. That said, it is true that apologetics did not seem as necessary from the moment Christianity became a state religion at the end of the fourth century. From that time period forward, individuals who dissented from the faith were forced either to emigrate or to conceal their dissent. It thus no longer appeared necessary for the church to develop a well-articulated rationale to persuade them to come to faith. Infant baptism had also become common, which meant that everyone was automatically assumed to be Christian. Even though the usefulness of apologetics was not denied, it was actually employed less and less.

In modern times, there have been several pendulum swings since the moment reason began to reign as "Queen" in European culture at the beginning of the eighteenth century. We observe from then on a very pronounced tendency on the part of Christian theologians to invest their energies in an apologetics that made an increasingly exclusive appeal to reason, deemed an autonomous faculty in itself, possessing its own law. All were in agreement to affirm: "We have to follow reason, for therein lies true freedom, and man's dignity." So they forced themselves to demonstrate that Christianity was compatible with reason. This was not achieved without difficulty, namely not without the temptation on the part of some to remove from Christianity whatever did not appear consistent with reason. The great philosopher Emmanuel Kant, in the eighteenth century, wrote a volume whose title is itself revealing, *Religion within the Bounds of Bare Reason*, for this was precisely the program he wished to promote. In reality, it made for a Christianity emptied of the core of its substance. But the Kantian endeavor was quite representative of the era: "reason" was on everyone's lips. Not long afterward, during the French Revolution, organized worship of the Supreme Being and of the Goddess Reason was even established. A fetching woman, a courtesan actually, was brought in to portray the Goddess Reason in the processions that ran through the streets of Paris. It is in the name of Reason that the Revolution itself found its justification.

In the eighteenth century, those who attempted to lead their contemporaries to faith readily emphasized a purely rational apologetics. The backlash was to come later. It appeared already in the great vogue of romanticism, which exalted that which does not appear rational in human existence: spontaneity, intuition, subjectivity. The far extreme of the challenge to the legitimacy of rational apologetics on behalf of these newfound sensibilities can be found in existentialist thought, and among those theologians influenced by it. In his *Christian Discourses*, Kierkegaard, a major thinker of the nineteenth century, would inflict a mortal wound to reason, declaring that he who invented "rational proofs for the existence of God" was another Judas! For the rationalist apologist betrays too, this time with the kiss of foolishness. Kierkegaard pits "true faith" against faith founded on rational logic. The former warrants taking a risk, like a "leap into the void," even in the face of contrary evidence. Kierkegaard vehemently rejected the notion that rational proofs should support the gospel. His thinking made an indelible mark on many twentieth-century thinkers, such as Gabriel Marcel, a French Catholic existentialist, who came to believe that "theodicy is atheism."[1] (For Catholic intellectuals, "theodicy" covers the whole range of attempts at establishing rational proof relative to God—his goodness, his existence—in spite of evil in the world.) In the Protestant camp, Karl Barth, too, fulminated against apologetics. Over the course of several decades, especially during the first half of the twentieth century, the general climate was deeply hostile to the very idea of apologetics, a posture which was completely out of step with the ancient tradition of the history of the church.

The evangelical movement could not help but be impacted. Among evangelicals, hostility to apologetics became wedded to certain notions inherited from Pietism. This seventeenth-century spiritual movement had played a role in many of evangelicalism's revivals and as such came to influence its heritage. Pietism, it will be remembered, had a tendency to oppose "heart" and reason. Evangelicals often embraced this dichotomy, which meant that reason was regularly sidelined in their conception of faith. For them, to believe was to cast aside proofs and arguments.

Evangelicals and Apologetics

On the other hand, if we move from the particular French situation to consider that of evangelicals worldwide, we observe a remarkable fact: it is precisely in the field of apologetics that

---

[1] *Journal Métaphysique* (Paris: Gallimard, 1927), 65.

evangelical Christians have broken new ground in the twentieth century. In dogmatics, relative to the interpretation of doctrine itself, some work has certainly been done, but there have been few truly original contributions. Just as well, perhaps, for it was mainly important to hold ground. As regards apologetics, however, new soil has been tilled. Some contributions were successful, others less so. It should be duly noted that two thinkers of the twentieth century were particularly important: Abraham Kuyper and James Orr. The former was a man of encyclopedic knowledge. He founded the Free University of Amsterdam and the Reformed Evangelical Churches of the Netherlands. He also served as prime minister of his country. He introduced new ways of thinking, concerning reason in particular. His insights and theses signaled a clear advancement in the understanding of biblical teaching. The latter was a Scotsman and professor of apologetics at Glasgow University. He defended the trustworthiness of the Old Testament against contemporary liberal theories and the Virgin Birth of Jesus against its deniers. He was also able to introduce a novel rhetorical style in apologetics, evincing brilliant skill. After these two men, a new generation of apologists stepped to the fore, which made its presence felt between the two wars and, in the United States, especially after the Second World War. Several different trends might be discerned in their teaching, but all aligned themselves in agreement behind the doctrine of the uncompromising authority of Holy Writ.

In the French-speaking world, little progress was made in apologetics until the beginning of the twenty-first century. We can only cite Francis Schaeffer, who founded the L'Abri ministry in Swiss Romandie. Although he carried out his ministry in English, it was in a Francophone setting. His writings were disseminated far and wide. While Schaeffer was influenced by the work of the two abovementioned evangelical apologists, and was also a former student of the "Kuyperian" Cornelius Van Til, he basically popularized the fruit of their labors. If he did not break much new ground in terms of content, he did create a highly original, and effective, apologetic language. Thanks to him, apologetics no longer remained in the Ivory Tower of specialists, but impacted seeking students and made veritable inroads into the general public. His ministry was remarkable in this domain. The writings of Francis Schaeffer represent the essence of what exists in French circles of evangelical apologetic thought. His works prove useful, given that his gift was to popularize and simplify. This also means that sometimes he wields an axe in places where others operate with a scalpel. . . . The specialist who reads what Francis Schaeffer has written in his own field of research may have the impression that he caricatures and oversimplifies. Such is the eternal struggle to balance the need to simplify for popularizing purposes and the desire to nuance in order to do justice to the complexity of thought from every viewpoint. In any case, Francis Schaeffer stopped in their tracks hundreds and hundreds of young people who were headed down the road of nihilism and suicide, if not literally, then at least intellectually and spiritually. Now, in recent years, we can also reference the Network of Evangelical Scientists whose works, the result of scientific and theological reflections, treat different aspects of the relationship between science and faith for a French-speaking audience.

The French Scene

The late French philosopher Jean Brun hewed to the Kierkegaardian tradition. Kierkegaard had championed Paradox (the heart of the gospel, as he saw it)—so it is only natural to find his relationship to apologetics paradoxical! On the one hand, Kierkegaard preached a faith that pledges itself against all evidence: the fewer the proofs, the purer the faith, for objective certitudes must be opposed. But what seems contrary to apologetic practice becomes transformed, in a certain way, into apologetics! For Kierkegaard made use of his *reason*. He was a towering intellectual. And all his efforts were aimed at conversion! It was so that his contemporaries might make the leap of faith that he elaborated his thought in commending Christianity to them! He praised Christianity above all other religions because Christianity—and Christianity alone!—demands faith in paradox. This is scandalous for reason. Kierkegaard offers, as it were, this *reason* for believing: faith is opposed to reason. Other commentators before have noted the paradoxical nature of Kierkegaard's thought, for his is a subtle and upside-down apologetics.

In Jean Brun's work, there exists this paradoxical bent, too. He can rage against the simple use of logic, and for that matter against all scientific endeavor (especially in his book *L'homme et le langage*, in which he disparages scientific endeavor in favor of purely aesthetic and intuitive perception). But he, too, develops an entire system of thought, well worked out, derived from his extensive reading and long reflection. And he, too, bears witness, albeit in a subtle and indirect manner, to his faith in Christ. As a philosopher, he did not move in theological circles. If he drew close to evangelicals and made common cause with them (or I should say *us*, for I have been the beneficiary of his warm society), it was because he perceived, through intuitive insight and his masterly understanding of the patterns of history, the emptiness of thought that predominates in contemporary culture. Alongside that emptiness, he also perceived, in his own Reformed tradition, the hollowness of liberal theology. By way of healthy reaction, and because he loved the Bible, he has offered us very useful help. As a dear friend, I would not take him as an intellectual guide—as a guide in the elaboration of Christian doctrine or apologetics—but rather as an unwitting defender of the faith. I am thankful for his articulate use of language, his sensitivity to layered and multifarious facets of reality. He has an uncanny knack for being able to appeal to a large readership among the cultivated class and to predispose them with a favorable perspective toward faith. He has remained, however, unclassifiable among the philosophical schools in academe, and thus somewhat isolated on the French scene.

Jacques Ellul, for his part, is an open and avowed Barthian, which is to say his work is heavily influenced by Karl Barth, with whom he was very close. Barthian theology (which is sometimes referred to as "evangelical") deviates appreciably from evangelical doctrine in the usual sense of the term (i.e., orthodox). Barth failed to recognize that Scripture *is* the Word of God, at all times, in all circumstances, whether we understand it or not, and therefore everything Scripture says must be received with total confidence, for it can neither induce us to error nor err itself. While Barth may also have called Scripture the Word of God, for him it was not intrinsically so, but only when God speaks to us through it. If sometimes he does appear to go further, he characterizes the Bible as the Word of God only in a loose sense, as the privileged locus where God produces the Event of his Word—where and when he decrees, irrespective of all human striving, since man-made religion *contradicts* divine self-disclosure. Barth could retain then the modern critical approach to the Bible, which he had learned from his liberal masters—even if he downplayed its importance.

Jacques Ellul showed himself to be faithful to Barth in that he, too, insisted on biblical authority. He often chose the most conservative readings in debates over biblical criticism, though he himself proved incapable of completely embracing orthodox faith. Ellul is especially useful to us in his analyses of different theological positions. He was a prodigiously versatile critic, as sharp-eyed as a lynx in detecting vulnerabilities in argument. He was known to critique evangelical thought with a fine-toothed comb and the results were not always flattering. At other times, though, he seemed to side with orthodoxy. His critique of certain ecumenical theologians, of Marxism, or of the current hands-off treatment of Islam whose power continues to fascinate, was of rare verve. He had great love for the Bible, which kept him from straying too far afield. He thus remained attached to central core beliefs. In his eyes, the divinity of Christ was never in question, and in that respect he adhered firmly to his Reformed confession. Unfortunately, he taught with the same vim and vigor the heretical doctrine of Universalism. He firmly believed that all will be saved in the end—a false hope the Bible obliges us to denounce for what it is.

The Fundamental Question

After this brief historical overview, let us now come to the heart of the matter. What is at issue? It seems that whether we rely on reason to lead human beings to faith (or to confirm them therein) or whether we dismiss reason altogether, we come up against some extremely serious difficulties. Whether we choose one path or the other, we are faced with hard questions to resolve. We find ourselves in a double bind, a veritable dilemma.

The Difficulties Attending Reliance on Reason

If we rely on reason, if we attempt to construct arguments to lead to the faith, it seems as though there is the great danger of falling into *rationalism*, which subordinates the Word of God to human deliberation. If we rely on arguments, does not reason become the ultimate authority by which all things are judged, including the Revelation of God? We decide then, based on our own reasoning, whether we are going to accept Divine Revelation or not. We put ourselves in the judgment seat. Is this position tenable? Herein undoubtedly lies the major danger that arises when we seek rational arguments to lead to faith. As I have already mentioned, history, and the eighteenth century in particular, shows us that many theologians caught up in rational arguments came to eliminate from Christianity that which conflicted with their reason.

The other difficulty concerns the *role ascribed to the Holy Spirit*. What role indeed remains, if it is by rational arguments that individuals are led to faith? It would seem that the Holy Spirit no longer has a bona fide mission in causing them to pass from unbelief to authentic faith. Some believers fear that a Christianity founded on reason depersonalizes their relationship with God, and only leaves them with a purely cerebral religion. It is our entire being which is liberated when we gain access to the knowledge of the Lord, along with those aspects of personhood which are anything but reason: emotion, intuition, sense. Consequently, how do we conceive of a purely rational Christianity, constructed with the support of arguments? Such is the serious difficulty when we emphasize recourse to reason alone.

Another difficulty demands our attention: those in the past who have laid claim to reason have come to *some very different con-*

clusions, not to mention antagonistic to one other. In the name of reason, has not almost every thesis and its opposite been advanced? Has not every manner of doctrine been proposed—each claiming to have reason on its side? The result has been a dreadful cacophony. Is this not proof enough that reason is like the proverbial wax nose, that it can be formed into all shapes? In the final analysis, reason is not a very trustworthy guide.

The Difficulties Attending Refusal of Reason

On the other hand, if we abandon the search for a rational foundation for faith, if we follow Kierkegaard, if we make faith a matter of the "heart" in the modern sense—beyond what reason can perceive, and sometimes even contrary to reason itself since we must believe without seeing—there, too, we encounter some significant difficulties! The problem of *cacophony* poses itself anew, and that in a compounded way. For what people choose on the basis of what they "feel," or based on their intuition or based on an impulse that suddenly overcomes them, devolves into something even worse than affirming everything and its opposite! For they can maintain two mutually exclusive arguments at the same time, hold the most preposterous of positions, sometimes advance appalling absurdities—all in the name of what they "feel."

Another problem also arises relative to the *responsibility* of the act of faith and, by the same token, that of the *guilt* associated with the refusal to commit to faith. (This is indeed the same problem, viewed from two different angles, though each must be distinguished.) We are called to choose. We were created for acts whose responsibility we must assume. But if there are no rational arguments to undergird them, we have to "make it up as we go along"! We then act on the basis of what we fancy at the moment or what crosses our mind, or according to a sudden rush or vague feeling that prompts us . . . this is not conducive to responsible decision making. How can we give an account for the hope that is in us? The responsibility to which we are called, which derives from our status as created in the image of God, seems impossible to safeguard if there is not a single rational argument that can be marshalled in support.

In any case, it must be acknowledged: if there are no underlying reasons that lead to the act of faith, it is impossible to reproach a person for not taking that step. On what grounds can he be reproached for refusing to believe, if there is nothing which attests to God? How can we consider him to bear any guilt for refusing to trust Jesus Christ? If nothing impels, nothing condemns! More to the point, in our culture nowadays, if apologetics has bad press, and if the notion that faith has no valid rationale is widespread, it is precisely because this stance helps avoid condemning those who refuse to believe. Our contemporaries react very strongly to the idea that their unbelief could be culpable or condemnable. They want nothing to do with it! They are willing to tolerate that faith be proposed to them as an option, as one aspect of the panoply of the human experience, and they quite willingly allow us to speak to them about it, but the thought that they might be considered culpable for the act of not believing makes them indignant. As a result, they rule out the notion that there could be reasons that lead to faith.

The New Testament, however, is very clear. We are inexcusable for not giving to God the glory he is due. "Therefore you have no excuse, O man . . ." (Romans 2:1 ESV). God condemns as sin the refusal to believe: the Holy Spirit "will convict the world concerning sin . . . concerning sin, because they do not believe in me" (John 16:8–9 ESV). "Whoever does not believe God has made him a liar" (1 John 5:10 ESV). This is an important biblical theme. Obviously, we should not bring it up first thing in conversation. Christians must take into account, in all charity, the struggle that certain individuals have in understanding. Nevertheless, if we seek to reflect in a rigorous manner on the problem at hand, we must conclude that, for the Bible, faith and unbelief are not two equally free options, left up to human beings to decide. Human beings are placed under obligation to believe in their Creator, to render him the honor which is the act of faith. The act of faith is free in the sense that no physical or psychological constraint must be brought to bear. It is not free in the sense that it is "morally optional." The individual whose original vocation consists in responding to Truth and Good is unfaithful to that vocation if he refuses a grounded faith. God bears witness to himself, and if an individual rejects his testimony, he insults his Creator. This is part and parcel of what the Bible evokes under the name of "sin."

Getting Our Bearings

On both sides of the equation, then, there are difficulties! It is of no avail to split the difference. We resolve nothing when we settle for a compromise between two untenable positions. In the first place, what right would we have to do so? What right would we have to say: "We'll accept this bit here and that bit there, since both are flawed"? We have not even established that the union of the two constitutes a satisfactory solution! Moreover, there remains the problem of proportion: Who shall say which bit of one position, versus which bit of another, is the right amount to take? The simple strategy of avoiding two pitfalls, since we have seen that there are (at least) two, does not suffice. We must find, if possible, a more solid position.

We make some headway, though, by delving into what must be said, based on biblical teaching, about both irrationalism and rationalism.

1. The first useful point to remember is that the very people who inveigh against reason and against the efforts aimed at rational analysis *use their reason* to do so. We have already made this remark with regard to Kierkegaard. But this is a widespread problem. There are no two ways about it: either people resort to vociferations and fist pounding, insisting that "It has to be this way because I say so, because I want it so, so there!"; or they attempt to justify their position. But as soon as they attempt to justify their position, without settling for antics and histrionics, it is to reason that they must appeal. Often, those who speak against reason render their task more difficult, because they have a very narrow conception of what reason is: for the most part, they reject *a type* of logic, *a way* of using it, *a certain style* perhaps. Such a misconception misleads because

it is so limiting: for to reason is to attempt to prove, and to prove with *all* the means available for truth-finding—which could bring about conviction in a person and lead him to say: "Yes, that works, that's consistent, that makes sense." If we point out to those who rail against reason that they contradict themselves, that annoys them, of course. Indeed, it is impossible for an individual to live life in any responsible manner without seeking to justify his choices through establishing necessary relationships: "I profess B, and to justify B, I have to find an A with a necessary relationship to B: if A, then B. If then I find A, I justify B." That's how we operate as humans. To operate in this way is to use reason! And reason does not have to be divorced from the facts, for the reason which the Bible encourages is based on the evidence of experience. This evidence, in return, can be the object of rational study. All of us, in the management of our daily lives, likewise use reason. If not, we would not survive very long! On what grounds, then, do we cease employing reason at any given moment? Reality itself displays a certain unity, in its very diversity, which can be explored. It would be capricious to suddenly hold back. We can, nay we must, make the exercise of our reason more flexible when our biases would curtail or inhibit it, to account for the reality we encounter. In broadening our minds, we do not abandon thereby the principle of rational self-examination with respect to our actions and thoughts. In order to remain truly human, we must not settle for capriciousness, for blind chance, or for emotionalism which suddenly overcomes us. We must try to connect our choices, without contradiction, to actual things.

How, too, can we *submit to the authority of Scripture* without using reason? Even Luther, who elsewhere had very harsh words to say about reason, declared at the Diet of Worms that he would not change his convictions unless it were demonstrated to him "by the testimony of the *Scriptures* or by clear *reason*."[2] It is noteworthy here that Luther speaks of "reason" (using the singular in the original Latin) on this solemn occasion. His point is well taken: we should

---

[2] *Faith and Freedom: An Invitation to the Writings of Martin Luther*, ed. John F. Thornton and Susan B. Varenne (New York: Vintage, 2002), 20.

not simply cite a verse in defense of our positions: it is also a matter of knowing how to apply it, how to draw conclusions from it. The process necessarily requires a certain use of reason.

It must be emphasized again, in view of the irrationalism which permeates a large segment of our society, that we cannot lead a responsible life without using reason, and that it is radically arbitrary to suddenly stop and say: "I'll reason to this point, yet no further."

2. Another, even more pertinent, consideration is that of *the biblical example*. If we systematically examine what the Bible has to say about the intellect or reason, we discover that, nine times out of ten, it is spoken of favorably. The Bible advocates its positive use. A few passages appear highly critical, to be sure, but that criticism, too, must be qualified. It is not just any reasoning or any understanding that God accuses of "folly." It is the understanding of "the wise of this age"! It relates to a world corrupted by sin. All too often, evangelical Christians have believed that it was simply the intellect or reason in themselves that were denigrated or condemned. In closely reading these biblical texts, however, we realize that nothing of the sort is the case: for reason and intellect are referenced more often than not in a positive light.

Indeed, in Scripture, we can see Jesus and the apostles availing themselves of logic and rational arguments. Matthew 12:27 records the rational methods used by the Lord Jesus himself, exposing an internal contradiction in the argumentation of the Pharisees, when they accuse him of driving out demons by Beelzebub. He reproaches them for the inconsistency of their reasoning. Similarly, on several occasions Jesus employs the *a fortiori* argument "how much more" (see Matthew 7:11). We discover the same rhetorical device in the Epistles. Moreover, the verb "to reason" often recurs in the book of Acts (if we take, for example, this possible translation of *dialegomai* in 17:17 or 19:8–9; cf. Apollos in 18:28, who *refuted* by *showing*). Paul uses logic to reproach the Galatians for seeking to return to the law: "for if righteousness were through the law, then Christ died for no purpose" (Galatians 2:21 ESV). The word "then" marks the articulation of a definite theological argument. There are two possible systems of righteousness, either through the observation of the law or through Jesus Christ, who takes all our sins and dies in our stead. Because of this clear distinction, the person who relies on obedience to the law to be pleasing to God must consider at the same time, in principle, that the death of Christ would not have been necessary. If he considers that system A (righteousness through the law) would have worked, "then" he must consider that system B was not necessary: "Christ died for nothing." Paul draws this conclusion in a rational manner. The person who would refuse the very idea that reason could be rigorously determinative would miss the crux of the apostle's argument, here in this passage and elsewhere. We thus have biblical models which run counter to contemporary irrationalism.

It must be clarified here that the notion of "heart" in the Bible corresponds generally to that of the intellect, contrary to what most readers today believe.[3] I shall return to this point later.

3. Finally, to what can be attributed this great wave of irrationalism in our culture, everywhere around us, since the romantic period? Why have so many been eager to decry reason, while, in everyday life, they must have recourse to it? We can single out two main causes.

The first is the *fatigue* that individuals feel, precisely because they employ their reason every day, in their work, in their day-to-day dealings. Unquestionably, this involves discipline. Discipline, generally speaking, does not occasion leaps of joy. It gives rather the impression of a burden. Since society has become extremely complicated, having developed an internal logic of its own in its very complication, due to rational work, the need for rational discipline in everyday life weighs ever heavier. For the peasant of long ago, he only needed his intellect to till and sow his field, and that wasn't too complicated. The disciplines of modern life have become much more demanding. As a result, a backlash has taken place: tired of reason, the world of today exhibits, for almost everything else, a kind of antirational explosion.

---

[3] See "Le coeur fait le théologien," in *Henri Blocher*, vol. 1, La Bible au microscope (Vaux-sur-Seine: Édifac, 2006), 11–24.

The second explanation, linked to the first but nevertheless distinct from it, is that modern man would fashion himself "without God nor Master." He declares "I." In asserting his individuality, he claims to be creator—and speaks often of his "creativity." He does not abide the notion that an order might be imposed on him, and in particular on that which matters most to him, on that which is the most intimate part of his being. He is obligated to submit himself to rational discipline for day-to-day affairs, but he considers these dealings more or less "outside" of his true self. For that which concerns the essence of his existence—his inner freedom—he does not want to be subject to an imperative which he himself has not initiated. He wants nothing to do with things that are, in a manner of speaking, "prescribed." Now reason itself, which may be wielded pridefully—and all the more so when it is wielded pridefully—is just as much an order which *imposes itself* on the human person. "If A then B, I must acknowledge it." It, too, is contrary to idolatrous self-assertion, where the "I" legislates of its own accord without any superseding law. It is fundamentally this self-promotion of the human subject, of the human "I" which puts itself on the supreme throne, which explains irrationalism, or the refusal of reason. For reason implies discipline; as such, it imposes submission. Therein lies the deep mystery of contemporary irrationalism.

This does not mean, however, that we should resort to rationalism, or the exaltation of "reason for reason's sake." There are, on that side of the ledger, many things to say as well, which will be the object of the next chapter.

2

RATIONALISM IN THE
LIGHT OF SCRIPTURE

As we have seen, the New Testament calls us to give an account for the hope that is in us. Jesus and the apostles, setting the example for us, practiced a kind of apologetics.

Two very serious pitfalls present themselves when we consider the use of reason on behalf of faith, either through excess or deficit. On the one hand, overreliance on reason seems to exclude or to diminish the role of the Holy Spirit and to reduce faith, which issues from the heart, into a conclusion based on a compelling argument. This is unacceptable. On the other hand, the refusal to make use of reason opens the door to everything and anything, and renders arbitrary the choice that makes us disciples of Jesus Christ. At the same time, it excuses the refusal to follow Jesus Christ: if there is no argument that leads to faith, that obliges faith, we do not see how the unbeliever could be judged for having rejected the invitation.

The data of our common experience, confirmed by Scripture, exclude irrationalism, which has become the dominant system of belief in our culture, most notably when it comes to art, philosophy, literature, and personal behavior. Indeed, if Scripture denounces reason, intellect, or striving after wisdom, it is not in themselves, but "according to the world," according to the norms and the perspectives of this present evil age. It is the "disputer of this age," the scholar "according to the basic principles of the world," whose folly God condemns (1 Corinthians 1:20; Colossians 2:8 NKJV).

We must now consider objections to rationalism. If irrationalism is excluded, rationalism does not any more conform to biblical teaching. Experience, too, can help us see that rationalism does not stand on solid ground.

Rationalism

What is rationalism? The subject can be elusive. It is important to clarify for ourselves a working understanding of the notion at the outset of our inquiry. Some label it rationalism as soon as there is any recourse whatsoever to reason. This use of the term is inappropriate. To be reasonable is not to be a rationalist. To be rational even is not to be a rationalist. We must distinguish among terms: rationalism is the idolatry of reason. A rationalist is a person who seeks to make reason his *only* guide in all the questions which he must decide. Rationalism treats human reason as an absolute, deems it autonomous, self-regulating. For the rationalist, reason is not subject to any higher authority, for it alone is the final judge. Reason is considered to be "standing on its own," by virtue of itself, first and last, reigning sovereign over all! This is why we employ the term idolatry.

The Observations of Experience

Rationalism seems excluded first by the data of experience. We can, of course, always debate this point—which is why we must always turn to the Bible for certainties!—but experience already sensitizes us to the failure of rationalism.

1. First of all, there have been *blatant disagreements*—for millennia—among those who claim to adhere to reason. If reason were a sure guide, possessing its own law in itself, then rationalists should all be able to fall into line! Now, it is clear that they are incapable of doing so. Were all their opinions to be taken together, it would be the worst of cacophonies. The rationalists' dream is to treat every subject in the same manner as mathematics. This has been particularly true since the seventeenth century, though

already Plato had the inscription "Let no one ignorant of geometry enter" placed above the door of his Academy. Indeed, in mathematics, discussions apparently end in agreement. The strength of the demonstration is such that there are no opposing factions: there is no "left-leaning mathematics" nor "right-leaning mathematics" whose partisans declare each other "anathema." In mathematics, at least, they arrive at a conclusion! There exists in the depths of man such a need of unity and certainty that the dream arises that everywhere it should be like mathematics, that rigorous reasoning might lead to conclusions beyond all challenge. Spinoza, for example, composed his main work—entitled *Ethics*, though it is his entire philosophy—in the manner of a geometric treatise: definitions, theorems, conclusions, "QED."[4] He thought he had reached unassailable conclusions . . . but other philosophers rose up, with other points of view. The followers of Reason, who had sought to make it *the* means of guiding man in all his endeavors, found themselves in opposition to one another.

2. As other critics have pointed out, once we observe *the way in which human reason functions*, we soon recognize that it is not autonomous. The assessment of a fact by reason and its very perception are themselves easily inclined in one direction or the other. It was most especially Pascal—a mathematical genius, inventor of the calculus of possibilities, among other things!—who in the seventeenth century first underscored this dependence regarding our entire affective life, if not physiological. In one particular passage, he pokes fun at the Great Thinker, for whom a mere fly, buzzing around his head, can prevent him from thinking! The man who would "reshape the world," and a mere fly causes him to make a mistake in his mathematical equations. . . . If a rationalist retorts by arguing that reason should only be judged by its own processes and that a distraction occasioned by an external factor does not prove

---

[4] Translator's note: From the Latin phrase *quod erat demonstrandum* ("thus it has been demonstrated"). The initials are traditionally placed at the end of a mathematical demonstration or philosophical argument to signal the completion of a proof.

its intrinsic weakness, it nevertheless remains true that *in practice* we can scarcely trust ourselves to a guide so sensitive to worldly and bodily interferences!

Also noteworthy is the *role of tradition* in the way in which we judge things. Our reason is tremendously influenced by its socio-cultural conditioning. Again, Pascal underscores this point: "Truth on this side of the Pyrenees, error on the other side." From community to community, country to country, matters which seem evident to the reason of some appear as impermissible errors to others. All it takes is moving a few kilometers. This conditioning due to many different factors, which pertains to the intellectual life, has been pointed out before, and it gives the lie to any claim to the autonomy of reason.

3. We can take it a step further still, with a more recent finding, which was hardly noticed before the twentieth century, but whose seed Saint Augustine had already planted. More and more researchers have realized that, even under the most controlled conditions—when all affective filters have been removed and the "personal equation" of the thinker has been kept at a minimum— *reason can never free itself from a certain number of assumptions,* of preconceived ideas, with which it must contend and which it is not capable of generating on its own. So, reason is not a law unto itself, it is not autonomous. Lucien Goldmann, one of the major figures of postwar Marxist thought in Paris, writes in his great work on Kant's philosophy: "The clearest result of the long methodological controversies of recent years has without doubt been to demonstrate the existence in every scientific or philosophic work of premises for which the author makes no attempt to provide a logical foundation."[5] It is impossible to establish rationally the premises which are assumed at the outset of reasoning. As I like to say, using a simple image, reason is like a mill which can only grind the grist which it is given. Reason needs presuppositions to be able to function properly and to produce anything at all.

---

[5] Lucien Goldmann, *Immanuel Kant*, trans. Robert Black (London: Verso, 2011), 50.

It is most interesting to note that even in mathematics, where the role of presuppositions appears the least obvious, the lack of autonomy of reason can be demonstrated. It can be demonstrated in three ways:

A. It is demonstrated when we question the *meaning of the words* that we employ. "Two plus two *equals* four." Does everyone agree? If such is the case, then everyone must mean the same thing by "equals." But if we pose this question, we realize that the defenders of rationalism differ. Their agreement is only on the surface. They employ the same term, but it does not mean the same thing, really and truly, for each and all. For some, it is a generalization based on experience. For others, it is a decision that they lay down: they decide that two plus two equals four. For still others, it is a truth contemplated intellectually, a "mathematical essence" that itself exists. Schools of thought conflict on this subject. Some would argue that it is perhaps not a question here of mathematics, but of the *philosophy* of mathematics. We cannot, however, separate the two, for again we have to specify the meaning of the word we employ. Does not the meaning of words depend on the proposition we formulate? Even in mathematics, agreed understanding on this score which every mind is compelled to ratify has not been reached.

B. It should then be noted the place of *presuppositions, postulates, and axioms* which mathematicians have discovered to underlie all their work. Even those who engage in elementary mathematics know that there are postulates which cannot be proven. Euclid's postulate affirms that, if a straight line falling on two straight lines make the interior angles on the same side less than two right angles, the two straight lines, if produced indefinitely, meet on that side on which the angles are less than the two right angles. This cannot be proven. Two other non-Euclidean geometries were developed on the basis of different postulates, either with a multitude of possible parallels or with none. One of them served Einstein in his theory of relativity.

What does not seem to play out on the level of our daily existence and common experience, of Euclidean-type (at least approximate), does seem to play out for the infinitely small or the infinitely great. One mathematician, Kurt Gödel, has even demonstrated that the canon of propositions of the most formalized mathematical system shall always remain incomplete. An undecidable proposition can always be formulated through its own means, though it is impossible to be grounded in itself.

C. In a highly interesting book (*Foundations of Christian Scholarship*, under the direction of Gary North), Vern Poythress, a theologian who also holds a doctorate in mathematics from Harvard, contributes a chapter on mathematics in which he demonstrates that *religiously oriented presuppositions* intervene in certain mathematical questions and incline the mathematician's thought in one way or the other. Poythress notes, for example, that Indian metaphysics, which denies multiplicity, normally renders mathematics impossible. Now, it is a religious decision to admit the reality of multiplicity. Biblical revelation endorses, in fact, this viewpoint, and the fundamental thrust of Indian thought stands in opposition to it. In the final analysis, it is the biblical doctrine of the Trinity which can ground the use that common mathematical thought makes of numbers, with its notions of plurality and unity.

Biblical Teaching

Biblical teaching confirms to us that treating reason as autonomous is tantamount to indulging in a fatal illusion, not to mention ungodly in many respects.

1. We must first of all stress the *theme of the "heart"* as the organ of thought. If we classify the texts of the Old Testament describing the functions attributed to the heart, those which are intellectual in nature are the most often evoked. The heart is the core of the thinking person. In the book of Proverbs, we often find the expression

"who lacks understanding," as one of the ways in which the fool is characterized. Literally, it is "who lacks heart." The translation "understanding" is not inaccurate here, though the Hebrew word (there are two forms, *lev* and *levav*) is elsewhere translated "heart." The notion has now evolved in meaning. For us, the heart is the seat of affections. This was not the case in previous times when it referred to courage ("Rodrigue, do you have heart?").[6] In the Bible, the heart is first the locus of the intellect, then of the will, and clearly later, that of emotion. In the Gospels, if the inspired authors who record the words of Jesus specify that loving God with "all your heart" is to love him with "all your mind" (for example in Mark 12:30), it is because in Greek, "heart" especially evoked "courage." It was necessary to add the latter term related to the mind so that the Greek readers might fully understand.[7] In Jeremiah 31:33, the prophet proclaims to the Israelites that God "will write his law on their hearts." In Hebrews 10:16, which quotes this passage, after the word used to translate "heart" the inspired writer adds the Greek term for "understanding" (in 8:10, the reversed word order confirms their equivalence). This detail is significant, for the heart is not only the seat of understanding; it is also the locus of the will, while emotions, too, play a role. This fact precludes reason from being considered a separate entity. In a sense, we might say that there is no "reason," only people who reason. There are only "hearts," or "interior beings," who are complex networks of intellectual, volitional, and affective functions. Confronted with their world, confronted with the data of experience, humans endowed with a heart seek at once to distinguish objects and their components, to grasp them together, to seek the connections linking them. These are

---

[6] Translator's note: The quotation is from Pierre Corneille's tragicomedy *Le Cid* (1636).

[7] In the text of Deuteronomy 6:4 cited by Jesus, the expression "with all your mind" does not occur, though it is implied in the Hebraic notion of "heart." Jesus would have cited the text in the original Hebrew. Apparently, the gospel writers who, under the inspiration of the Holy Spirit, wanted to render in Greek the meaning of his words, thus specified "with all your mind."

the two main functions of the mind and they are inseparable: to discern and to understand; namely, to identify necessary relationships. We comprehend and our reason is satisfied when we are not content to see that two things follow one another, but see why it was *necessary* that they follow one another. It is this necessary connection that reason seeks. When reason has seized it, it has acquired a knowledge that stands out from the present moment. It knows that the sequence will occur again, since A necessarily brought about B.

2. A second biblical given, and of paramount importance, is the theme of *the darkening of the mind* in the life of the unbeliever, or his inability to comprehend the things of God. The theme is found in several passages: "The natural person does not accept the things of the Spirit of God" (1 Corinthians 2:14 ESV). Paul also speaks of the "darkened understanding" of unbelievers (Ephesians 4:18 ESV), or of "their foolish hearts [being] darkened" (Romans 1:21 ESV). If the mind were an autonomous faculty, it does not follow that merely being an unbeliever, or a worshipper of Jupiter or Baal, would affect the mind. We have here then the formal pronouncement that the mind bears the consequences of the choices of the heart in matters religious.

3. Another biblical theme is of a piece with the preceding one, to wit, the doctrine according to which *God must impress an orientation* on the heart of man for him to think aright, for his intellect to be sound, for him to appreciate what should be appreciated. Already, in the Old Testament, the foundational proverb affirms that "the fear of the LORD is the principle of wisdom" (Proverbs 1:7). Often this verse is rendered "the beginning of wisdom," but "principle" is more exact. It is not simply a matter of starting from scratch, but of the principle which presides for the duration. The fear of the Lord is the respect for his Word, it is the complete submission to his Lordship. The New Testament, for its part, speaks of the "renewing" of the mind (Romans 12:2), and asks us not to conform to this present age, with its ideas, its scales of value, its structures of meaning, its matrices through which phenomena are interpreted, and without which reason is not supposed to function. In Ephesians 4, when Paul speaks of the darkened understanding

of the pagans, he invites us to be transformed "in the spirit of your minds" (Ephesians 4:23 KJV), which is to say in the orientation, the driving power of the intellect. This corresponds to the "fear of the LORD" in the Old Testament.

On What Basis Can There Be Dialogue?

A question then arises in apologetics: If the mind depends for its functioning on presuppositions, on underlying sets of values, and on unspoken criteria, and if the presuppositions of the people we meet are not those of Scripture, what use is it to dialogue? There is no longer any common ground. Is not the task of apologetics rendered impossible by these antirationalist conditions?

1. One tempting solution is to resort to a kind of *compromise*. It assumes there still remains in man some unaffected vestiges which suffice for entering into dialogue. This would be the common ground on which we can stand to begin discussion and to go deeper from there. But this solution is fool's gold. It is quite true that the darkening of the mind in natural man, yet to be regenerated by the grace of God, is not uniform in every point. The distortion by the prism of the criteria and presuppositions of the world is not the same in every domain. It varies according to the culture, the individual, and the discipline. Thus, in mathematics, for example, it is not so drastic, and we can work fairly well and reason together. As a very general rule, the distortion becomes all the more acute as we approach the most delicate point, which is when a relationship with God is at issue. At that juncture, the distortion is at its peak. When we remain far removed from that point, the individual does not feel obliged to acknowledge God. Not realizing that this discipline, too, belongs to God and not feeling threatened in his assertion of independence, he has little to distort. The distortion is thus more or less serious in some disciplines rather than others. However, there is no domain completely free of it; everything is affected to a certain degree. We cannot therefore minimize the difficulty of postulating a neutral meeting ground.

2. The correct solution is provided by Paul in Romans 1. This text permits us to see where natural man stands with respect to the workings of the mind and their relationship to the witness of God. We have raised the issue of the interpretive prism used by natural man, which is contrary to God and which distorts his vision (2 Peter 1:9 speaks literally of "nearsightedness"). It is not the only factor in play. In the real world, God bears witness to himself: "For what can be known about God is plain to them" (Romans 1:19 ESV). God reveals himself through his works. Reality has a structure because of God. It has laws, relationships of meaning, and a form established by God which gives him glory. Natural man lives in this world which God has fashioned and which maintains the form that God has given it, in spite of the repercussions of the fall. In his very essence as a created being, natural man is made for God. Therefore, when he applies distorted criteria to his surroundings, *it is not all that simple for him*. It does not happen of its own accord. It is not as if he has at his disposal a soft wax which he can shape any which way. The manipulation takes energy out of him. Because he does *not* recognize the witness that reality bears to God, he must twist reality. It is not easy for him to kick against the goads of the world (cf. Acts 26:14). The apostle Paul says that man without God "holds" the truth captive in unrighteousness (Romans 1:18; the verb, in the original text, can mean either "detain" or "hold"). Humans have chosen their so-called independence from God; they do not want to give him glory, thus they suppress the witness which is everywhere around them, they divert it, they plaster it on their idols. A concerted effort is necessary for such a distorted outlook. It becomes a kind of struggle, when man seeks to distort the structure of things such as God has established them. There are times when that twisting "doesn't jive." Sometimes, it becomes necessary for him to bypass an aspect of reality. It is at this price that natural man applies his interpretive matrix to the world. He subconsciously experiences the difficulty.

What transpires when we enter into "apologetic" dialogue, when we propose an *apologia* to individuals who do not yet adhere to the gospel? We do not put ourselves on the same footing as the natural man left to his own devices, we do not adopt his presuppositions. We speak according to the truth that God has made known to us, by his grace. We emphasize the true structure of things: we highlight the witness that reality bears to its creator. As a result, it becomes *more difficult* for natural man who is in conversation with us to suppress and divert this witness, as he usually does. Where he would evade something, we bring it to his attention. At that point, one of two things will occur: either he will suppress even more, not wanting to understand, digging in deeper his heels—and our arguments are not going to overcome his hardness of heart!—or the Holy Spirit will use the arguments that we employ and will impress upon him the structure of reality such as God has created it, whereupon his defenses will break down, the distorted perspective will dissolve, and he will become open to other ideas, notably to the idea of God. This is what the New Testament calls *metanoia* (conversion), which is "another way of thinking" (the word comes from the root of the word "intellect, reason"). Herein lies the essence of apologetic argumentation. We must not think that arguments alone suffice. If our interlocutor barricades himself behind presuppositions that are contrary to those of God, our arguments will make little headway with him. He can very well close himself off from them. If it pleases God, though, they can still serve as a tool of the Holy Spirit.

How Long to Persevere?

How long should we persevere in "apologetic" dialogue? From a practical standpoint, two realities should be underscored.

1. As the degree of perspective distortion differs among individuals and from place to place, we must always *adapt ourselves to the interlocutor*. Our first objective is to "surprise" him. With respect to the system he has established (the spiritual-intellectual lockbox which keeps a lid on his feelings of insecurity), we must awaken what he has suppressed and unsettle him. This is what we hope can *destabilize* the distorting system by which he holds truth

captive. Where there is little distortion, we can get a foot in the door and raise questions, as does Paul in Acts 17. The apostle makes use of the assertion—albeit somewhat veiled and pantheistic: "We are his offspring" (Acts 17:28 NIV). He builds on it to query his interlocutors as to their idolatry: If you recognize that humanity is God's progeny, why do you make gods out of stone and wood? Paul points out the contradiction, and he does so in taking into account the audience he has before him. Addressing Stoics, he cites the words of a Stoic poet.

2. Another practical consideration: What is it that may cause our interlocutor to feel, when we present our arguments before him, that it would be difficult to continue in his distortion of reality? He assimilates this thanks to that uncanny ability which our mind has to "touch" the mind of the Other. When we speak to one another, a kind of connection is established, a *spiritual connection*. We mimic in our own thought patterns the thoughts of the Other, which touch us. It is in this same way that our words in conversation do not remain simply external to our interlocutor, but awaken in him what he had tried to suppress. However, this phenomenon of spiritual communication, which exists between individual humans, is greatly facilitated, nay multiplied, when there is a positive affective environment, for it is the heart of man as an entire being who thinks. When it is a trusted friend who presents this brand-new thought, it penetrates more deeply, it is more difficult to dismiss, than when it is a stranger or a disagreeable personality. Personal relationships, therefore, have a large part in apologetics.

Such is the promise that God makes to the apologist, to the humble and courageous disciple who seeks to persuade with serious arguments the brother or sister in our common humanity. Liberated at once from rationalism and irrationalism, the mind renewed by the Word can *touch* the mind of a conversational partner—something which the Holy Spirit can use in turn to liberate him through the knowledge of Truth for Life anew.

3

REFLECTION ON AN
OBJECTION TO THE FAITH

"YOU CAN MAKE THE BIBLE
SAY WHATEVER YOU WANT"

After having considered the problem of the relationship between faith and reason, let us turn now to a particular topic in apologetics, and which relates to a frequent objection to the Christian faith.

It goes without saying, we cannot have an answer for everything. There will always be some gray areas. We should not be made to feel uncomfortable, much less guilty, if we are not up to the task of resolving all the intellectual difficulties that individuals of good or bad faith throw at us. We are neither omniscient nor infallible. There will always be gaps in what we know. With respect to certain questions, it is impossible to have even an informed opinion given the current state of research today.

We should not therefore feel obligated to propose an intellectually satisfying answer to every question that arises. On the other hand, we can attempt to offer answers that are as detailed and as tailored to the situation as possible.

At the same time, we must banish from our minds debilitating trains of thought. Often we are reluctant, unless we have acquired sufficient expertise in a certain domain, to speak up or to engage in dialogue. "I don't want to give the impression that the Christian faith can't be adequately defended," we say to ourselves, "I don't want to run that risk." The fear is paralyzing, and it is not likely to get any better, for the more we learn about a given field of study, the more we realize just how vast it really is, and that we have little time to bring ourselves up to speed.

The business of learning and becoming informed is not optional, and the energy thereby expended is not in vain, but we must not *overestimate* its importance. Acquiring knowledge is worthwhile, in the final analysis, as a simple instrument in God's hands. Perfectionism, which indefinitely holds us back from witnessing and engaging in apologetics, betrays an excessive preoccupation with the *self*, when all should be grace. It is grace which moves and convinces. It is grace which works miracles with the incomplete and more or less well-constructed arguments we propose. God's power is made perfect in our weakness.

Jesus entreats his disciples to exclaim, *after* they have fulfilled his commands, that they are but "worthless servants" (Luke 17:10). Worthless, yes, but not *useless*. Although Christ could very well do without our services, he desires for us to participate in his work. He overcomes then our weaknesses and deficiencies. He invites us to engage in dialogue and he himself promises to give us, when necessary in his eyes, the supernaturally inspired answer we need (Matthew 10:19–20). In some instances, it could be that our confession of ignorance will have more of an effect than a proper and sound answer. One day a science professor, who was a believer, wanted to witness to his colleagues about his faith. As he did so, he became all tangled up in his notes, making himself look ridiculous in the process. Paradoxically, that made a positive impression on one of them. He later came to the gospel, drawn by the fact that this man, on the same par as he, was willing to risk his reputation amongst his peers in order to bear witness to his faith!

While acknowledging, then, the limits inherent in the quest for *good* arguments, let us come straightaway to the objection raised against our faith which deserves priority consideration. In logical order, the question relative to the source of knowledge, to the ultimate authority, naturally arises first. On what grounds do we assert what we assert? Evangelical Christians accept Holy Scripture, God's Word, the Touchstone of our witness, and rely on it to "guarantee" what we affirm. Now, our interlocutors readily quip: "You cite the Bible, always the Bible, yet the Bible . . . you make it say whatever you want! So many different people get all sorts of contradictory things out of it! Your authority, then, doesn't amount to much!"

The teaching of the Bible, as this objection would have it, is ambiguous, while Christians maintain that it is not. If it is ambiguous, it cannot serve as a reference. This objection, if it were well founded, would be devastating for us. For if it were true that the Bible allows for mutually contradictory doctrines, the testimony of Christians would no longer have much meaning. They would find themselves totally disarmed in their apologetics. They might offer up a personal, purely subjective testimony, but it would elicit on the part of their interlocutors little more than a shrug or a smile. It would be something quite different than the truth of the gospel, to which our faith holds fast. Let us not be ignorant: this objection to Christianity revolves in the minds of many around us. As early as the sixteenth century, it was making the rounds. The Bible was likened to a "wax nose," as the popular expression would have it, a kind of Play-Doh to which could be given one form or another.

We can distinguish three "tiers" in the examination of this question. In the first instance, we must address the multitude of *versions* that conflict and vie with one another, all claiming to be "the" Bible. In the second, we must answer the objection according to which the Bible would consist of elements *so diverse*, nay so contradictory, that each person can pick and choose what suits him. In the third, we must consider the *integrity of the biblical text itself*, which some declare to have been "tampered with," reworked from one generation to another, over the centuries. The Bible today, in their contention, would be the product of a kind of sedimentation, with successive corrections, additions, and subtractions by editors who all were not in agreement amongst themselves, or who passed along errors in copying.

The Transmission of the Biblical Text

Let us first address the "third tier," the question of the integrity of the text. At issue: the work of the copyists, and more generally that of the "editors" (as they fulfilled their role in ancient times), in the transmission of the sacred writings.

Doubts as to the quality of the "copy" that has come down to us may trouble the minds of some, though very few amongst those really in the know. The difficulty is removed when we become aware of the historical facts, about which almost all scholars are in agreement. C. S. Lewis was a professor at Oxford University and, without doubt, the most prodigious Christian apologist of the last century. He served in the army during the First World War and, while rubbing shoulders with men less educated than his former university colleagues, had occasion to take due note of the main cause of skepticism amongst many with respect to the Bible. To his great surprise, it was not, as he had initially thought, the question of miracles that gave them pause, but the fact that the biblical texts were so ancient.[8] It appears that the transmission process in a time period so far removed from our own would engender, amongst those with a nonliterary background, a vague but deep-seated distrust. Such old writings must have been poorly copied, modified, or tampered with! It is this objection we must meet head-on. Yet C. S. Lewis found the following answer effective, knowing that, for our contemporaries, Science has become the irrefutable Reference, the fail-safe Guarantee (we are not far here from idolatry). In order to reassure them, he explained that there exists a ready-made science for determining, at least in all probability, the authentic biblical text: it is the science of textual criticism. Once it was understood that scholars treat the matter methodically, *scientifically*, that they spend their careers collating manuscripts, ascertaining their value, refining the rules that help them to recover the most plausible form of the original text—henceforth practically certain—that is what seems to have been persuasive, that is what removed a false difficulty on the path to faith.

---

[8] C. S. Lewis, *God in the Dock* (Grand Rapids: Eerdmans, 1970), 94.

The Text of the New Testament

We do not bend a knee in scientific idolatry if we emphasize that a discipline called textual criticism indeed exists. All those who practice it, whatever might be their own faith commitment or theology, arrive at roughly the same conclusions. For the New Testament, in any case, we have every reason to believe that we possess, practically speaking, the original texts. We do not have, to be sure, the original manuscripts of Tertius, for example, who wrote under the apostle's dictation (Romans 16:22), though the manuscripts we do have in hand, numerous and overwhelmingly consistent, have lost nothing from the autograph copy (as it is termed). Comparing these many manuscripts together allows us to reconstitute the original text, so that we can say, with the highest degree of probability, that we have *essentially* what Paul dictated. For no other ancient writer, such as Plato or Seneca for example, do we enjoy as favorable a set of circumstances. For no other writer are there as many manuscripts as close in time to the composition of his work. This fact alone should allay any fears. Frederick F. Bruce, a great exegete of the twentieth century, who closed his career as professor of a prestigious chair at the University of Manchester and who presided for a time over the International Society of New Testament Studies, briefly and simply presents these conclusions in his short book: *The New Testament Documents: Are They Reliable?*[9] His work, irreproachable scientifically, and which has not been contested, has the wherewithal to dispel, with respect to the New Testament, the concerns that have been raised.

The Text of the Old Testament

For the Old Testament, it must be acknowledged that the situation is not as straightforward. The Old Testament was composed well before the New Testament, and our earliest manuscripts, except small fragments, are those that have been discovered in the caves

---

[9] F. F. Bruce, *The New Testament Documents: Are They Reliable?* (Grand Rapids: Eerdmans, 1967).

near the Dead Sea. These caves had served as the hiding place for
the library of the Essene monastic community of Qumran, where
the extreme dryness of the climate permitted their preservation
until 1947. These first documents are several centuries later than the
composition of the books by the original biblical authors. The most
ancient texts, after those of Qumran, only date from the Middle
Ages. There is thus a significant lapse of time between their original
composition and the earliest surviving known manuscripts.

We cannot *prove* in the same way as we did for the New Testament, with the same degree of scientific probability, that the text
which has been transmitted to us by the extant manuscripts is like
the very one which Moses or the prophets Isaiah or Jeremiah origi-
nally composed. We must acknowledge some leeway and a lesser
degree of certainty.

Two considerations which carry some weight, however, must
be taken into account with respect to the preservation of the Old
Testament text:

A. First of all, we must emphasize that there exists no adverse
evidence. If the Old Testament situation is "less favorable" than
that of the New Testament, due to the five-hundred-year in-
terval between the two, it does not therefore mean that there
must be *un*favorable evidence. No one can prove that large-
scale corruptions, modifications, or interpolations have found
their way into the manuscripts. Christians need not then feel
ill at ease. The situation is normal. Because centuries have intervened, about which we know precious little, it is impossible
to prove either the reliability or the possible unreliability of the
textual transmission.

B. On the other hand, we know that the work of the scribes
was carried out with the greatest care. Because the Israelites
recognized that they were dealing with sacred writings, they
went about their reproduction with extreme diligence. They
dutifully abstained from any additions to the text or any subtractions from it. The Jewish historian Flavius Josephus, in the

first century after Christ, says so expressly in his book *Against Apion*. During certain periods, at least, every single letter of a given biblical book was counted, and if a copyist did not come out to the exact number of letters expected, instead of looking for the error to correct it, the entire copy was burned. This just goes to show the extreme measures that were brought to bear to safeguard the transmission of the biblical text. We find another indication of this effort in the treatment of obvious errors which appear in some verses. Some occur, for instance, when a letter is mistaken for another, much like a typographical error in a printed work today. Such errors are easily corrected. However, in the Old Testament (which the Jews call "Tanakh"), such errors are not corrected *in* the text. The editors responsible for the transmission of the Scriptures decided instead to put notes in the margins (the technical name for such a note is *tiqqūn sōferīm*, "correction of scribes"). They venerated Holy Writ to such an extent that, after having received a text containing an error from a preceding copyist, they did not feel at liberty to emend it, even in the face of obvious evidence. It was a sign of their extreme respect for the heritage to be handed down that they refrained. In spite of this vigilance and rigor, some errors—of rather minor importance for the overall meaning—may have occurred in some passages, for God did not endow copyists with infallibility. The larger point here is that extreme measures were taken so that the received text would not be tampered with.

The Successive Editions/Versions of the Text?

When the notion of "transmission" is broadened to include editorial revisions—that is, deliberate modifications to the text with a view to modernizing it, prophecies reworked so as to harmonize them with their ultimate fulfillment, deletions sometimes, or more often additions of short phrases between lines (interpolations)—on these things the opinions of the "experts" conflict, even drastically.

Flavius Josephus' statement in his *Against Apion* excludes the possibility of these editorial revisions unequivocally. The most rigorous evangelical specialists rely on his testimony and follow his
authority. Quite to the contrary, for the overwhelming majority of
biblical scholars outside of evangelical circles, higher criticism has
been *the* established practice. For them, the prophetic books, for
example, would be the work of schools, accrued over the course of
several generations, rather than that of individuals whom Tradition
holds to be their authors. An early prophet, at first, only handed
down a portion of what later came to be transmitted in his name.
Then, his disciples, imagining they were being consistent with him,
added some oracles—a first generation, then a second, if not a third.
Sometimes, these disciples changed the entire orientation of the
original message: a prophecy which had in view a single event was
adjusted to accommodate yet another. It is in this way that many
higher critics today attempt to explain the process of composition
of the books of the Old Testament, so that Flavius Josephus, arriv-
ing centuries later on the scene, is an unimportant witness in their
eyes. Those who resist the prevailing thesis (or rather we should
say "hypothesis"), in general those who are committed evangelicals,
but also some distinguished Jewish authors, note that it can only
be based on considerations of *internal* criticism. If the modernist
contemporary biblical scholar finds disparities in the received text,
he supposes they are the product of different hands. He tires of the
redundancies in certain passages and suspects the conflation of
parallel documents, even though they differ somewhat. He assumes
that predictions could not have been made—miraculously—two
centuries in advance, etc. It is *because of these factors* he sees the
hand of later editors other than the original author. What could be
more subjective? Does he not project onto the biblical document
his own contemporary writing practices? Does he adequately take
into account the writing methods and the literary conventions of
the ancient Middle East? His myopia in not taking into account the
available objective data would become even more acute were he to
consider the treatment of sacred books in the surrounding coun-
tries in the Mediterranean world. Nowhere else was a text believed

to be inspired by the gods given over to revision by later editors. Such is the compelling argument advanced by an expert on the subject, renowned Egyptologist Kenneth Kitchen, who taught at the University of Liverpool and is the author of several important books. In taking due note of the contributions of archeology to our understanding of the Old Testament, he excludes the hypothesis of successive editors on the basis of the known practices of scribes and priests in the neighboring lands.

The Bible, a Contradictory Book?

The second tier in the objection to faith concerns the existence of contradictions within the Bible. For a great number of theologians, it goes without saying that the Scriptures contain contradictions: James and Paul disagree, for they would seem diametrically opposed on the subject of justification. Some find discrepancies in the treatment of the virgin birth of Christ: while Matthew and Luke would appear to be "for" the doctrine, John and Paul would appear to be "against" it. Some maintain that all the sacred writers contradict one another in one way or another throughout the entire Bible.

The Role of Presuppositions

It is impossible to understate the importance of this factor. It goes straight to the heart of the matter with respect to confidence in the authority of Scripture, both in principle and in practice. The limitations of this present study do not allow for entering into the details of the debate. I should like, however, to highlight a truth too often disregarded; namely, the disagreements on this topic do not proceed from a disparity with respect to *knowledge*, that is, relative to the consideration of archeological, historical, and philological data. Evangelical Christians who admire the internal harmony of the entire Bible are not less competent than the theologians or biblical scholars who find contradictions in it. What makes all the difference is the attitude within at the outset, with its preset opinions and presuppositions, its mental framework and implicit criteria, its "worldview" (including or excluding, among other things, its belief in the supernatural).

How might the determinative role of presuppositions and pre-set opinions be demonstrated to an outside observer?

A. It should be remarked that the theologians and biblical scholars who believe they find contradictions in the Bible are not in agreement amongst themselves. This fact speaks volumes. It would not be surprising if it were only a matter of details or of minor issues. In every discipline, there remain certain disagreements amongst researchers. But here it is a matter of fundamental issues, of entire viewpoints that are in opposition. And this is demonstrably so. On specific questions, we find contrary views on the part of equally distinguished academics. A Scandinavian school of thought holds to the *oral* transmission of data leading to the composition of the Gospels we have today. On the other hand, for another school of thought, in Germany, this transmission was effectuated by means of brief documents which the "editors" cut up with "scissors" and "glued" together according to the arrangements that seemed preferable to them. If such approaches are in contradiction, it is not a question of knowledge, of facts that some individuals might know and that others might not. It is rather a question of choice, of mental attitude adopted from the get-go, of ideological perspective and philosophic influences.

B. Moreover, it bears repeating, the hundreds and thousands of evangelical specialists who affirm the theological coherence and uniformity of the entire Bible hold the same scholarly credentials as their higher criticism colleagues. Many of them earned their diplomas at the same universities, where they distinguished themselves just as brilliantly, and participate in archeological work in the field. They cannot be caricatured as marginal eccentrics, as flat-earthers are with respect to cosmology. They are too numerous, having professionally organized themselves into guilds, producing a regular output of high-caliber scholarship that demonstrates their familiarity with opposing viewpoints. Although they suffer, broadly speaking, from an unjust discrimination, on less polemical subjects they publish works whose quality liberals themselves commend. I think of authors such as Donald Carson or Greg Beale. . . . One need only meet them to see that they bear all the reassuring marks of at least an average mental health. Their resistance to higher criticism cannot be attributed to personality quirks or to a specific neurosis.

Let every exegete now enter the lists of biblical scholarship, armed with the awareness of the presuppositions he holds (and why!).

The Diversity of Interpretations

We come at last to the "first tier" of the argument against faith—to the problem of the disconcerting diversity of interpretations of the Bible (actually, the question of contradictions implies it already). This variety of interpretations is observable in the sects and the great branches of the Christian tradition, which all officially claim to base their doctrines on the Bible. The question also arises with respect to Judaism and even extends to Islam. How do we cope with such a multiplicity of interpretations?

1. A preliminary remark—yet by far the most important—must be made in order to answer these detractors. What exactly are these competing doctrines that are said to differ, though all basing themselves on the Bible, and which seem to imply that the Bible can be made to say whatever one wants? About which groups are we speaking? And how do they invoke biblical authority?

If we take a little closer look, instead of settling for some vague notion of universal confusion, we come to realize that those groups that clash in referencing the Bible do so because they appeal to *another* authority besides the Bible. And they readily admit so, based on their own particular approach as they themselves define it. If their theological compass is not the Bible alone, if they take their cue from another guide, and if this guide is not the same for the different competing sects, nothing is more "normal" than for them not to be in agreement. The Bible should not therefore be blamed for divergent views, since it alone is not taken as their guide. Conclusions are different among groups because the claimed sources of authority differ. To blame such a discrepancy on the Bible is just evidence of lack of rigor in thinking.

2. It can often be observed, for example, that sectarian movements fundamentally differ amongst themselves due to the special revelations which the founder of the given sect claims to have received. These "illuminations" determine both the approach to faith and the understanding of that faith. They go well beyond the scope of the Bible, and are much more determinative in terms of the spiritual formation of the sect's followers. If Mormons disagree with Jehovah's Witnesses, it is because Mormons accept as foundational revelation, in addition to the Bible, and even more important than the Bible, the so-called golden plates discovered by Joseph Smith (the *Book of Mormon*). As for Jehovah's Witnesses, they always cite the revelations of their founders, in particular Charles T. Russell, or his personal insights in the interpretation of the Bible, and so on and so forth.

Broadly speaking, sects tend to arise when an individual with a strong personality and great charisma has the conviction that God has revealed uniquely to him or to her the true meaning of Scripture. Others before have not succeeded in perceiving what he now is privy to by supernatural means. Sometimes, in addition to coming up with peculiar interpretations of Scripture, he might attribute to entire books a "second Bible" status. In all events, whether the sect is based on some special revelation or an appeal is made to some supplementary text, the framework remains the same: another authority is made to supersede the Bible, and that new authority is considered more absolute. Hundreds of cults have arisen this way over the course of church history. The individuals who founded them may well be endowed with eloquence and personal magnetism, if not a semblance of holiness, for they might be devoted to others or leading an ascetic existence, all of which impresses. They might also be helpful, and appear able—for a time—to resolve the problems of those who come to them. And so, they draw converts. All the while an authority other than that of Scripture is used to elaborate a new doctrine. In such cases, we should not be surprised, then, if sectarians arrive at different conclusions. It is not the Bible itself which holds sway over them, but rather some outside influence, and which proves decisive in terms of their spiritual commitments.

An analogous situation exists historically with respect to the great divisions within Christendom. One of the major debates of the sixteenth century was centered on the role of tradition, and at stake was the understanding of the controlling authority in biblical interpretation. The officials of the Holy See refused to recognize the principle of *sola scriptura* as their touchstone. At the Council of Trent, they defended as church dogma the notion that the faithful needed both the Bible *and* Tradition. It is not so surprising, then, that Catholics and Protestants might have arrived at different interpretations of the same biblical passages, since the latter would only follow Scripture, whereas the former have allowed themselves to be guided, in the final analysis, by the determinations of the Roman Magisterium. The conviction on the part of Catholics that they are thereby more faithful to Scripture changes nothing. *Pragmatically* speaking, there remains a duality of controlling authorities in Catholicism, which means that the Bible itself, contrary to those who claim it is like the proverbial "wax nose," is not the source of opposition between Catholic doctrine and Reformed doctrine.

As for Catholic conviction (Roman in the West, Orthodox in the Byzantine East and Russia) that *another* authority is not added to that of the Bible, we must look beyond semantics to facts. In all sincerity, Catholicism asserts: "The Bible is the Word of God, the supreme authority; only, to truly apprehend it, we must live with and within the church in which resides the Holy Spirit, we must humbly allow ourselves to be led by Tradition, which articulates what is not explicitly stated in the Bible, and by the Magisterium that God has established." This position is respectable, though it would only have probative persuasiveness if it derived from an *independent* inquiry into biblical teaching. Otherwise, it begs the question, and stacks the deck. Catholics believe themselves faithful to Scripture because they say Scripture confers this role to the Magisterium, but it is only Scripture in return *as interpreted by the Magisterium* which confers this role! It is at least easy enough to see that *two* expressly distinct authorities are in operation, as the traditional doctrine of the "two sources" of revelation (Tradition and Scripture) would itself suggest. More to the point, even if the authority of Scripture is deemed *theoretically* superior, according to Catholic teaching, that of the Ecclesiastical Magisterium takes precedence in practice, since it decidedly dictates what the true meaning of Scripture must be. How can the Word of God (which, according to Hebrews 4:12, is said to be the mediating *kritikos*) fulfill its role as arbiter of the Magisterium's decisions? Catholicism shifts the primary locus of the faith to the church, as the custodian of Divine Truth. The very term "Magisterium" derives from the word "master" and suggests the supremacy of the prerogatives claimed by the church. In the final analysis, it is not Scripture which is guide and master, it is the church which is mother and teacher according to the title of one of Pope John XXIII's encyclicals (*Mater et Magistra*).

That said, the fabric of interpersonal relations often softens the effect of strict doctrinal rationales! On the Catholic side, we know that the pronouncements of theological officialdom are not always respected by the rank and file (which might assuage some Protestants!). Many Catholics challenge more or less openly the Magisterium itself, either on the basis of biblical truth which speaks for itself—for the Word of God is not fettered—or due to the influence of ideologies foreign to the Catholic tradition. By the same token, evangelicals who like to adorn their banners with the slogan *sola scriptura*, "by Scripture alone," uncritically allow themselves as well to be shaped by external influences.

3. That branch of Protestantism which goes by the name "liberal," by its own admission, does not appeal to "the entire Bible and only the Bible" as its final authority. Its adherents clearly claim that they respect the Bible—they read it, even more than their core principles might allow, which is always curious to observe—but, at

the same time, they declare that they are not bound by *everything* the Bible affirms. What serves then to guide them? Their personal intuition, feelings dictated by their private experiences, the consensus of their community (affirmed as an "identity," and hence inherently legitimate), or what they believe to be the latest advancement of Progress. . . . It does not take much to recognize here the telltale mark of certain philosophies in their intellectual milieu.

Liberal Protestants, as well as "modernists" in the Catholic ranks, value the Bible and want to honor it, all the while privileging de facto the judgment of the reader over biblical teaching—because they think they detect errors and other infelicities in what the inspired authors have written. According to their lights, all the different findings which the sciences have been able to gather together must serve as a guide at the same time as the Bible, and in order to sift what is true from what may be false. At best, the most conservative among them attribute differing values of truth to the various propositions they might find. They choose what appears to them to be the most probable reading—based on their intuition, their community loyalty, and, more often than not, what they esteem to be the most rational, the most scientific. Clearly, in adopting this approach, they set up another fundamental authority taking precedence over Scripture. This, then, authorizes them to determine on their own what to retain and what to leave by the wayside. It is ultimately left up to them to ascertain the nature of doctrine.

Under the name of liberalism or modernism, this approach has become the majority position in Christendom today. Great thinkers such as Montaigne and Pascal, however, were able to see that reason is pliable every which way, that it only operates according to the unarticulated assumptions that direct it. We cannot ignore this fact when we consider the history of liberalisms and modernisms. "Reason" which is invoked and superimposed on the Bible is always determined by the philosophical school in fashion at the time. History, since the eighteenth century, we can now say with hindsight, shows that the successive prevailing philosophical trends each had their theological schools. Liberal theology tends to follow philosophy.

Thus, Hegelian philosophy gave birth to Hegelian theology; existentialist philosophy gave birth to existentialist theology. Wave upon successive wave: dogmatic rationalism in philosophy, followed by Kantian critical rationalism, was reflected in theology, after which Hegelian, existentialist, neo-Marxist, and "postmodern" theologies arrived on the scene. The phenomenon confirms for us the fact that "reason" does not have a separate existence. Only humans reason, and do so under the influence of the various philosophic trends at the time.

It is not surprising then that the theological conclusions of different groups—their doctrinal interpretations and positions—differ. As soon as another authority comes to play a key role, Scripture cannot be accused of being ambiguous simply because various people understand it differently. The Bible has not been, of course, jettisoned by liberals and modernists, for they vaguely sense that if they discarded it entirely, nothing of their theological system would remain. However, the authority of philosophy or the authority of science (itself often imbued with ideology) now determines the ultimate meaning of the Bible. The plethora of approaches for interpreting Scripture and for formulating doctrine goes a long way toward explaining the current cacophony of theologies and teachings. How can dissonance be avoided when so many follow such a great number of conductors at the same time and tune their musical instruments to such different tuning forks?

Agreement on the Essentials

In order to truly accuse the Bible of not being clear and of not furnishing a firm set of standards to those who seek such a set of standards, it would be necessary for those who say they do take the entire Bible and only the Bible as their final authority to have profound disagreements amongst themselves. Is such the case? We can say no. It is a demonstrable fact: those who hold the aforementioned attitude toward the Bible tend to be in agreement on the main points, thus on the essentials. They would subscribe, for example, to the statement of faith of the World Evangelical Alliance and thus hold in common a certain number of cardinal truths. Nuances remain here and there, which is undeniable, but a general framework is recognized.

Given this context, the Bible cannot be made to say whatever one wants. Scripture is sufficiently clear (the church fathers were wont to speak of its *perspicuitas*) for everyone to agree on the "high articles of the divine majesty" (Luther) which concern the Trinity, the divinity of Christ, his virgin birth, his bodily resurrection, salvation through his atonement, the gift of the Holy Spirit, and the Second Coming.

The Differences That Remain

Why do differences nevertheless remain?

A. We must always remember the fallibility to which we are all subject. How difficult it is for us to submit ourselves to a truly rigorous approach! We are all inclined to accept what flatters us and to approach topics in the way that suits us. In our daily dealings, the misunderstandings that arise often reflect errors of interpretation influenced by the nonintellectual factors that impinge upon our emotions.

B. More pertinently, we must stress the utter absence of exegetical method on the part of scores and scores of Bible readers, even the best intentioned. Many do not read the Bible as they would, for example, a professional manual in the workplace. They read the Bible as if it were a kind of electrical field. They "pinch" here and they "pinch" there in order to receive an electric jolt. Sadly, by way of contrast, when they study for their work, they do so by closely reading the text, forcing themselves to understand the writer's intention, taking due note of the important points so as to grasp the writer's line of reasoning, going back again and reading over when they do not understand—in other words, they go about the task methodically, *seriously*! But when it comes to the Bible, they have no method at all.

C. More pertinently still, there are certain presuppositions which, even for those with an otherwise solid evangelical faith, can reorient their viewpoint by just a few arc-minutes, so that they miss perceiving what had been intended.

The Wisdom of the Written Form Chosen by God

When all is said and done, there remain relatively *few* theological differences, when we take into account our fallibility, our ignorance, our hasty manner of reading the biblical texts, and how we sometimes tease out of them the meaning that we want. Lastly, it is remarkable that such a solid agreement prevails in terms of the essentials. We would do well to appreciate this blessing from the grace of God, who cherishes his children and prevents them from going too far astray. I believe the form that God has chosen for the Bible is especially pertinent. If the Bible had been composed in a systematic manner, like a treatise or manual in which topics are treated once and only once, in perfect order, it would have perhaps saved some space! It would have also rendered the interpretation of the text more susceptible to error, for a skewed perspective would not have been able to be corrected. God preferred a more dynamic and varied means of revelation. If there do indeed exist in Scripture some systematic expositions (the Epistles to the Romans and Hebrews for example), they are rather abbreviated and are embedded in a broader context. The Bible presents itself as a living organism: the same subject is reprised again and again by authors with diverse personalities, at different periods. When we fall into error in one place, we can correct ourselves in another. What we thought we had understood in one passage, we can reexamine in the light of another. For the topics that come up less often, the risk of misapprehension and hence of disagreement is ever present, but God in his wisdom has seen to it that the essential matters are treated fairly often, so that, in spite of our myopia and our clumsiness, we can all see clearly—insofar as we have a mind to submit ourselves as disciplined disciples to biblical authority. Multifaceted variety is what God has chosen for his Word, which accommodates itself to every human social condition and which lends itself as well to self-correction.

We might compare God's chosen method of revealing truth with the different ways a social engagement might be chronicled by means of photography. One could attempt to do so with a group shot, with all the partygoers neatly arranged in well-spaced rows. One could also take a wide array of snapshots, inside the crowd, from different angles. It would be these photographs taken from various angles, at different moments, which would be the truest and the most accurate record of what actually transpired. We should be indebted to God for the lively and diversified way in which he has chosen to communicate to us his revelation throughout the entire Bible. It helps us to come to agreement over the essentials.

The Main Areas of Disagreement

What might be said about the painful conflicts that nevertheless remain? We must understand their origin and their nature. From whence arise disagreements? Sanctification is an ongoing process; we have not yet attained our goal; we have not yet entered into the fully restored kingdom. The apostle Paul, writing to the Philippians, did not yet consider himself to have attained the prize, but strained forward to seize it (Philippians 3:13–14). This has nothing to do with his apostolic teaching, for within the context of his mission-ary mandate for the church, he was protected by a special grace that guaranteed him from theological error, as other biblical texts confirm. But with respect to his personal understanding, he was not infallible. In his process of working through the teachings for which he was a messenger on our behalf, he might have committed errors: "I am still not all I should be" (Philippians 3:13 TLB). He does not claim to be pure from all sin in his life (cf. 1 Corinthians 4:3–4). According to the apostle John, if a man says he has no sin, he is only fooling himself (1 John 1:8). Christians remain, while still on this earth, sanctified in only an imperfect sense. And that imperfec-tion affects our understanding, for the dynamic of our inner being is such that we cannot disassociate reason, will, and imagination.

We continue to be affected by the vestiges of sin within us, by the sinful world which surrounds us and whose influence we are inevitably subject to. We, too, are beings of our present age. Accordingly, we do not perceive in all accuracy the totality of Scripture. We are likewise influenced by certain philosophical trends, without really even realizing it. We are, alas, prone to the commonest of errors: drawing hasty conclusions, picking and choosing what pleases us, rejecting what suits us least. Evangelical Christians do not err in such an overt fashion, for they would deny the faith that they profess. Without realizing it, though, they overlook the verses that bother them or which are not in line with their own thinking. . . .

It might be said that there are three domains in which rather major conflicts persist amongst those who subscribe to the principle of *sola scriptura*—setting aside the essentials which are safely assumed—conflicts which are not inconsequential. It seems to me that, in each one of these areas, we can find an explanation for how disagreement arose.

The first domain relates to ecclesiology. How do we define the church? How do individuals become members of the church? Should the young children of the faithful to be automatically considered members of the church or not? This is an issue that divides believers. No doubt, sociological reality impacts greatly how the question is handled. Theological reasoning and biblical interpretation are influenced by this factor, which explains in large part the occurrence of divergent views. If we call into question the structures of this "society" which is the church, if we have to overhaul them, the task is too arduous, the cost too high, for it would cause upheaval within families! As a result, the temptation is strong to adapt our understanding of biblical texts to more practical and livable necessities.

The second area has to do with the doctrine of *divine election* (in other words, the predestination of the elect to faith and to salvation). The question could not be more important, and yet evangelical Christians are not all in accord. The dividing line that separates them one from another is of an entirely different nature than that of the ecclesiological divisions. It has to do with the difficulty that many have to wrap their minds around fundamental notions such as free will and responsibility. The more we routinely refer to an idea, the more foundational it becomes for us, hence the more difficult it is for us to say what we mean by it and to correct the conception of it that we may have assimilated. If something concerns a matter of secondary importance, such as a technical concept linked to work, we can revise our thinking and reform our comportment. If it concerns a notion that delves into the very essence of our being, it is all the more difficult. Which is why we must appeal to brotherly and sisterly tolerance when convictions clash over election and predestination, over free will and responsibility.

The third domain is that of *eschatology*, or the doctrine of last things. There, too, we observe sharp conflicts amongst brethren of good will. We can identify at least two reasons which serve to explain how they came about.

A. The figurative language—to a lesser or a greater degree according to the interpreters—which the Bible employs to speak about this issue. The apocalypse is an encrypted genre, deliberately encrypted. It is therefore not surprising that we should be less in agreement on its meaning than on other matters.

B. The only viable test that can sift out the veracity of eschatological interpretations is what actually takes place in the future. Consequently, we are not always able, in the present, to refute the visionaries who invent elaborate theories. Differences in this domain can never have the endorsement of experienced reality, so they are limited in their scope. They do not, in any case, endanger the essentials of the faith—what is necessary to know, not only to be saved, but to walk with the Lord and honor him in this world, so that we might live in communion with our brothers and sisters.

We might add, in parallel to possible disagreements over the end times (eschatology), those concerning origins (protology) and the interpretation of the first chapters of Genesis (the Apocalypse of the first creation). Another area of sometimes unfortunate controversy has to do with the doctrine of the Holy Spirit and his work today (for example, is being "baptized in the Holy Spirit" a necessary second experience, after conversion to Christ? And how do we consider the "spiritual gifts" that accompany the work of the Spirit?). In this latter domain, it is the personal declarations of intense spiritual experiences that have stirred the most profound emotions, which then become the basis of discrepancies in interpretation.

In spite of these issues of contention among evangelical Christians, the Bible is not a "wax nose." We must take care not to treat it as if it lends itself to manipulations of meaning, not to twist it in whichever way we wish. We should apply ourselves, instead, to methodological rigor in order to draw closer and closer, individually and collectively, to what it says to us on God's behalf. Your Word is Truth!

4

RESPONSE TO THE OBJECTION

"SCIENTIFIC ENDEAVOR IS CONTRARY TO FAITH"

Amidst the storm, in the glory of his majesty, God reveals himself to Job. He finally responds to the patriarch's questions and fires back some of his own: "Where were you when I laid the earth's foundation?" (Job 38:4 ESV). This passage puts into proper perspective the systems of knowledge which human beings construct—the tower of their toil, the monument to their own intelligence, *and* the temptation of their pride. The brilliant philosopher François Châtelet (professor at the "counterculture" university first located in Vincennes, then in Saint-Denis, who, though Marxist in his leanings, kept an open mind) once made the clear-sighted observation that the scientific template regulates the intellectual undertakings of our civilization: "It imposes itself as the panacea, the way, the life, and the truth" (I recall his phraseology from an article or a magazine interview). Châtelet reprises here the famous threefold expression from John 14, recast in alliterative wording,[10] which makes it more forceful from an oratorical point of view. Many in society today, as Châtelet well observed, attribute to science what Jesus stated concerning himself. This epistemological shift stands as a supreme valorization of science,

---

[10] Translator's note: For "the way, the life, and the truth," Châtelet employs three words beginning with "v": "la voie, la vie et la vérité." In most French Bible translations, "chemin" is used instead of "voie."

and in opposition to the Christian faith. Our contemporaries seem to have more or less adopted this conclusion: if scientific inquiry now commands respect, it is no longer tenable to return to the old ruts of the Christian faith.

Modern Science

The word "science" simply means "knowledge." There were, before modern science, and there are today, apart from it, many real knowable things or those which claim to be so. But when our contemporaries valorize "science," they mean that particular branch of knowledge that developed and was elaborated in the sixteenth and seventeenth centuries, before it extended its empire to all of Modernity. This science is, without doubt, from the perspective of world history, the greatest distinctiveness of our Western civilization, and now it has become globalized. The place it now occupies in society, as well as the technology that issues from it, stands out when we consider our culture in comparison with every other.

Amongst the characteristic traits of modern science, we must note its *close association with technology*. Science brings about a new mastery of the world through the application of its discoveries, while at the same time becoming more and more dependent on technology in research. In order for scholars today to keep up with the latest advances in scientific know-how, they need facilities, equipment, and machinery of extreme sophistication. This only reinforces the association with technology that is characteristic of modern science.

There exist two other unique features of modern science not found in classical science.

The first is the *method of planned experimentation*. Historically, a certain know-how was always drawn from experiences one had and experiments one conducted. Historically, discoveries always arose from a certain contact with reality. We need only think of Archimedes and his "Eureka!" ("I have found it!") when, in his bathtub, he suddenly understood that the volume of water displaced must be equal to the volume of the part of the body that had been submerged. It was an experience, combined with a certain sharpness of mind, that led Archimedes to his discovery. Observation was *the* preferred method of classical science, which places it in close connection with experience. The innovation of modern science, which gives it its great fruitfulness, has been the method of *planned* experimentation. Learned men were no longer content to experiment haphazardly, they planned. Tests were conceived to verify a hypothesis, procedures were set up in a very precise way so as to determine a clear outcome concerning an hypothesis that had been formulated. By planning, experience gave way to experimentation. This had never occurred before. Of course, alchemists had tried, time and time again, to transform lead into gold, but their attempts were nothing like the meticulous and systematic planning that brought about the extraordinary progress of modern science.

The second characteristic trait is *the maximal recourse to mathematical instruments*. The work of modern science has been a work of formalization with the aid of mathematics, so as to put as many problems as possible into mathematical equations. Scientists began with what could be quantified most easily. These days, "human sciences," as they are denominated, endeavor to attain this same forensic status by adopting more stringent measures through quantitative analysis and mathematical statistics. Modern science, which can boast of extraordinary successes, has advanced thanks to this expansion of pure intelligence, which seems to be independent of the external world and to develop solely in the mind of the geometer or algebraist. The glories of reason!

I can well imagine the modern critic, or the debater of this age who sees in this type of scholar *the* mediator of Truth, standing up proudly in reply to the ironic query of the Lord in the thirty-eighth chapter of Job: "But, of course, I know the laws of heaven! I know how snow forms, I know all these things cited by the Creator."

Miscellaneous Objections

The difficulty in the task of apologetics, if we might reply to those who entertain such a lofty opinion of science and who imagine it to be incompatible with the Christian faith, derives from the great variety of objections that have been raised. They differ widely, according to the extent of information these objectors have concerning the sciences and the Bible. We encounter some arguments which are gross and simplistic, others which are far subtler. Some of the better-informed detractors readily repudiate the facile and common forms of opposition between science and faith, only to find another way of opposing them. The range of misconceptions relative to the incompatibility of faith and science thus extends from the most rudimentary to the most sophisticated. What to do? We must aim for a medium, addressing the entire "package" of multifaceted objections, to try to respond holistically. It should be borne in mind, however, that even when we level out the "topography" of the intellectual landscape, our approach—the register of discourse, the nature of the discussion, the particular aim—will still depend on the interlocutor.

If we attempt to identify the principle incompatibilities in the view of many of our interlocutors, they might be divided into three categories: 1) on the basis of principles, of methods, according to which the so-called "scientific" spirit is opposed to that of faith; 2) on the basis of outcomes; 3) the particular question of miracles, which merits its own treatment. We will concentrate on the first category in this chapter, reserving the other two for later.

Objections on the Basis of Principles

How does the relationship between science and faith, with regard to their respective principles and methods, manifest itself? The antagonism seems well-nigh absolute.

On the science side, there is ever an effort to broaden rational knowledge. Procedures are developed which, when experience and mathematics are conjoined, can lead to convincing proof, to incontrovertible evidence. This is what science properly strives for. In contradistinction, what is faith? It is a wellspring of trust that flows from the heart. Faith concerns precisely what cannot be proved. It is opposed to sight. It is the rejection of all tangible support derived from what can be touched, manipulated—those things which form the very foundation of scientific inquiry. We walk by faith, not by sight. Which means that we are faced with a head-on collision, a profound opposition, between scientific endeavor and faith as faith!

Faith involves the most intimate of commitments. It brings to the fore each individual's responsibility before God. On the contrary—and yet another antagonism that grafts itself onto the first—scholars strive for objectivity, they seek to formulate statements that will be equally valid for all other observers, they seek to rid themselves of what is sometimes termed the "personal equation." A researcher is a human being like everyone else. He can be given to negligent errors due to a passing fatigue. He can nurse biases based on his particular affective state. Hence the "personal equation." The scientific method sets out to eliminate the effect of this psycho-affective dimension. Objectivity is the aim. The faith journey, in contrast, seeks the greatest intimacy through a personal relationship with God.

Academics revel in methodological rigor. The scientific approach obliges them to question everything—in the first place, received ideas and anecdotal evidence. Academics are taught to accept nothing at first sight, to submit all to verification, to critique everything. One of the pioneers of modern science, René Descartes, as much a philosopher as a brilliant mathematician (he was the founder of analytic geometry), begins his *Discourse on the Method* by contesting everything he had learned, all the precepts he had inherited, and even the witness of the senses. The scientific method likewise consists in calling into question what had heretofore been assumed. The attitude of faith, on the contrary, accepts authority: it submits, it humbles itself in trust before the authoritative word. It is not onerous to do so precisely because faith is trust. But this posture is at odds with the critical method. The dichotomy is particularly clear-cut when it comes to evangelical faith. The faith of so-called "liberal" or "modernist" Christians, as we discussed earlier, is characterized by independence vis-à-vis the Bible. Indulging in such critical license seems to us incompatible with a *consistent* Christian faith. We view it as a compromise with the spirit of this age, and we believe we must resist any biblical criticism that sits in judgment over Scripture.

There is again an incompatibility with the scientific method itself. A fourth and fundamental opposition concerns the continuous reconsideration of the achievements of science. Many scholars, nowadays in particular, are wont to say: "There is no settled scientific truth, scientific truth is always provisional. We might be able to summarize the present state of a question, but we must fully admit that the facts as we know them could be overturned with advancements in research." Indeed, theories are elaborated, revamped, reworked, and when a theory is taken up again and again such that it no longer seems tenable, a sea change occurs: there is a scientific revolution, and a new theoretical paradigm replaces the former. There is thus no immutable truth regarding science. On the faith side, on the other hand, "eternal truth" is affirmed. There are enduring realities, though invisible, of the law of the Lord which itself does not change. Jesus Christ is the same today and eternally, his word endures forever. These notions stand in stark contrast with scientific principles and methods.

The True Nature of Faith

When it is *wrongly* believed that A and B contradict one another, it is either because A is misunderstood, B is misunderstood, or both are misunderstood. In the case of the intersection of faith and science, suffice it to say, objectors entertain false notions about *both* A and B. In order to redress the damage done, we must begin by correcting the distorted perceptions that are still commonly held about one and the other.

Let us first of all correct a misconception concerning faith. When some contrast faith with rational processes, they see faith only as an emotional overflow from the "heart," in the modern sense. This is a fundamental misunderstanding if we are talking about biblical faith. Holy Scripture never recommends a faith that would devolve into irrational escapism ("You're so lucky to have faith!"). The apostle Paul specifically wrote: "I speak as to sensible people; judge for yourselves what I say" (1 Corinthians 10:15 ESV). Biblical faith is based on *evidence*. Now, is faith itself "evidence" or is it more a "conviction based on evidence"? In the famous faith "theorem" found in Hebrews 11:1, translators opt for either one or the other of these two expressions. It is pointless to try to determine definitively here which is the best exegetical and philological reading. What is significant, though, is that demonstration or evidence is associated with faith. The association of the two is commonplace. Thus, in the book of Acts, it is written that the risen Lord presented himself to his disciples in multiple ways, and that he gave them "many convincing proofs that he was alive" (Acts 1:3 NIV). The apostle Paul, when exposing before the Athenian philosophers the role that Jesus will exercise as judge at the end of times, avers that God gave a "proof of this to everyone by raising him from the dead" (Acts 17:31 NIV). The notion that faith and evidence are fundamentally opposed is anything but biblical. Faith finds firm footing rather in duly attested facts.

Misunderstandings have occurred on this score for two main reasons.

The word "heart" has changed meaning (see chapter two) and is no longer employed today, in common usage, in the biblical sense. It signifies for our contemporaries the seat of the affections, and thus is opposed to reason: "Faith of the heart = irrational approach." In the scriptural sense, as we will recall, the heart is first and foremost the organ of thought and desire, as if it were the very center of the individual, the seat of the will and reason. Heart is rightly translated as "common sense" or "understanding" when it occurs in the book of Proverbs or in the book of Hebrews, for this is the true meaning of the word! That the heart is the organ of faith is evident in the Bible; however, faith is not reducible to mere emotional impulse. Faith entails a completely rational comportment (where the will has a large part). The semantic evolution of the word heart has led some people astray.

A second reason for opposing faith and reason, mentioned earlier as well, is the occurrence in the Bible of certain admonitions against the wisdom of this world as well as its claims to understanding (1 Corinthians 1–2). For quite a number of readers, in too great a rush to delve any deeper or adversely predisposed by the ambient anti-intellectual subculture within evangelicalism, the apostle Paul would oppose faith and knowledge per se, while condemning the use of reason. What Paul rejects rather is the corrupted intellect, functioning according to the philosophic principles of a humanity hostile to God and idolatrous of its own attainments. It is a mind led astray by pride that is opposed to the true wisdom of God. His wisdom alone makes us wise unto salvation, whereas the present age mocks it and treats it as "foolishness." In the Epistle to the Romans, Paul states quite categorically: "Do not conform to the pattern of this world, but be transformed by the renewing of your mind" (Romans 12:2 NIV). It is not a question then of dismissing the intellect or of taking refuge in a kind of comforting escapism. No, faith is an act solidly grounded in the evidence which the Lord provides through the revelation he gives of himself and his plans.

Neither credulity nor unbelief! Man hostile to God oscillates between these two pathological polarities. He refuses what God proposes to him in spite of sufficient proofs to convince him—for he girds himself against the Truth with layer upon layer of false reasoning. He renders himself disbelieving because, in his pride, he does not allow himself to be taught. At the same time, he lapses into a kind of "credulity," accepting what is patently incredible without evidence. Our modern era which boasts of so much rationality is also that which has witnessed a proliferation of charlatans and other practitioners of the occult. Some of the leading lights of our so-called intelligentsia have reportedly consulted astrologers on the sly. This foray into the paranormal is actually quite typical on their part. Biblical faith is at once opposed to the disbelief of the prideful man who asserts his own intellectual independence and to the gullibility of the man who swallows whole whatever he is told. Let us not mince words in denouncing such a persistent mis-understanding: Christian faith is really not so far removed from scientific enterprise, although their goals and means of access are distinct—and thus differences appear in their procedures.

The True Nature of Science

The opposition between science and faith proceeds as well, in certain cases, from a misguided conception of science. If biblical faith is not an irrational impulse, in parallel fashion, science is far from being a purely objective enterprise, as if reason were discon-nected from every other function of the human psyche. What we have previously set forth concerning rational processes on the whole can be applied here to the specifically *scientific* operation of the mind.

The image which many people have today of the scientific method, which is opposed to faith, is rooted in the nineteenth century and inspired by the philosophy of science of the time. It scarcely corresponds anymore to the real work of researchers nor to what philosophers of science now commonly acknowledge to be the scientific approach. This approach is marked by its fair share of subjectivity. Certainly, in science, it is right and proper to aim for objectivity: scientists cannot say whatever they want nor advance any thesis that they please. Still, subjectivity on the part of the re-searcher cannot be held at bay.

Thus, the researcher's "personal equation" comes into play, al-beit indirectly and depending on circumstances. His research will be modulated, as it were, in accordance with his own affective state, his private ambitions, or his rivalry with some or other laboratory, in the hopes of one day being awarded a Nobel Prize . . . or at least so say those who are versed in the modi operandi of the scientific community. The role that inner motivational factors play is not insignificant, although remaining wholly external to the scientific endeavor per se.

At the heart of the researcher's "personal equation" is the role played by the imagination, which history records as crucial in all breakthrough advancements. Numerous philosophers of science have highlighted this fact. Scholars are not merely "clinically objective" individuals who, because they have detected a reoccurrence within given phenomena, say to themselves by simple induction that such and such a law must be in operation. In actuality, the truly genius scholars are creative and imaginative. They may have observed a phenomenon occur once or twice before; then, all of a sudden, something clicks: "Hey, maybe that's it!" The proverbial apple that bonked Newton on the head would be a worthy emblem. A new way of perceiving what is already known arises in the irrepressible minds of these ever-curious researchers. They formulate a hypothesis, construct a model, often on still shaky ground. Then, they imagine—once again, it is the imagination!—what sort of experiment might be conceived so as to verify or to disprove the hypothesis or model. Karl Popper, a leading commentator on the scientific method, has stated that experiments are especially useful for *disproving* invalid hypotheses. When an experiment succeeds, a scientist can never be absolutely sure as to the reason why it succeeds, for there may be many different reasons. On the other hand, a disproof through experimentation can permit a scientist to affirm that the hypothesis is not valid and that another one must be formulated.

Imagination is the mother of hypotheses. It extends to the limits of its own horizons, according to the overarching parameters that the thinker allows. These parameters can never be accurately measured. To a large extent, they belong to the common heritage of the scientific community of the period in question. This is the reason why several scholars, in spite of the individualistic bent of their imagination, might discover something new at the very same time. Only, a certain number of conditions must first come together, so that the horizon of their collective scientific knowledge might be inflected in a certain way, for the hypothesis to appear feasible to them and thus germinate in their minds. Genius makes an inroad precisely because it perceives and produces an opening, but it is always only relatively new. All of this is at a great remove from the popular image of the scholar who would operate by simply applying purely dispassionate reason on the basis of previously recorded data.

The necessarily "subjective" dimension of the researcher's work is confirmed by the testimony of non-Christian scholars themselves. They readily admit, with refreshing frankness, that *science remains a precarious undertaking*, subject to personal passions and ideological manipulation. Science is not capable of making good in any credible way on its claim to objectivity. Einstein himself came to note that scientific research is just as subjective an activity as any other. His is a testimony that carries some weight! The esteemed ethologist Konrad Lorenz also clearly saw that scholars are not any more exempt than others from cultural biases. Many scientific theses are too plastic to be reproduced in a laboratory, and yet they are accepted like the whims of fashion, without the undergirding of any veritable scientific authority. And yet, the public at large imagines that it was *Science* that has spoken. In citing these household names as witnesses, as it were, against a field in which they are the most prestigious representatives, we can lay the groundwork to show those who oppose the integration of faith and science with upturned noses that the matter is not so simple.

The Faith of Science

Let us dig a little deeper, deeper than the modulating influence of personality, temperament, and the imaginative parameters of the ambient culture. At the root of scientific study, *presuppositions* must be taken into account, as we have seen with respect to mental processes in general and mathematics in particular. We encounter the same phenomenon in the natural sciences. The researcher can never formulate a hypothesis, conceive of an experiment, not to mention determine the result of that experiment, without building on a certain number of presuppositions. He needs some criteria to determine the end result. These are prior to the very formulation of his hypotheses. He does not leap into the void. He has a starting point, something he has previously established. Every system rests on a certain number of prior postulates or premises. At bottom, his is an act of faith. At the inception of the scientific undertaking, then, this act of faith is what presupposes that without which the undertaking is not possible or has no meaning.

But which faith? What is to be presupposed? Historically, at least, the matter is not in dispute. The celebrated philosopher Alfred N. Whitehead, also a high-level mathematician and professor at secular Harvard, was not the first to shed light on the subject when he opined: *the origins of modern science are Christian.* The phenomenon which is modern science could only have taken root and blossomed in the history of mankind in a single soil—the one in which Christianity exerted its influence, slowly but surely molding minds. A certain number of believing scientists played a major role in this regard, not least of which was Francis Bacon, in terms of defining the experimental method. (Bacon had been strongly influenced by the English Reformation in the seventeenth century, albeit through its more liberal strains.) It was in neither a Buddhist milieu nor an animist milieu that these developments took place. In these other civilizations, quite so, some scientific achievements did come about, but nothing like the march of modern science with its continual progress and accrued knowledge. The Chinese made some great discoveries, covered significant ground on their own—which is to be admired—but then they found themselves at an impasse, for their worldview did not permit them to establish the kind of ever-advancing science that has flourished in Christendom.

The planned experimental method could only have been conceived in a certain sort of world, a world that is neither enchanted nor magical, in which anything and everything can happen like in a fairy tale, but rather in a world that is regulated, that obeys laws, without at the same time limiting man to these laws. A world, then, whose system is not closed in on itself. If not, man would be, like other elements of the universe, only a cog in the machine, incapable of having the requisite overview that scientific research supposes. To formulate a hypothesis, it is necessary for man to place himself on par with the world, so to speak, and to be able to declare: "Things are this way or that way." His mind must function independently of nature, so that he might verify, then, through an experiment he has constructed, whether or not his hypothesis corresponds to reality. In order to achieve this balance, the world must have an intelligible order (were it to be chaos, experimental science could not take place), while rational man must have freedom with respect to this system to which he himself belongs. In a word, man must at once be in the world and remain detached from the world.

These conditions can only come together within *the context of the biblical worldview*. With the conception of a God who is above his creation, who established patterns and laws, who placed man on earth with the vocation to bear his image, and endowed him with the needed faculties to fulfill this vocation. As God's response to Job in the midst of the storm or as Jeremiah 31:35–36 reminds us, God has set limits and established patterns. The biblical universe is not capricious. Pagan gods are capricious! The God of the Bible is the most sovereign and trustworthy God, whose creation everywhere bespeaks stability. As for man, he is not only, as an earthbound creature, subject to the laws of physics, he is also capable, as the image of God, of rising above them in order to view them and recognize them as they are in fact. By participating in the wisdom of the God who created him, man can say "yes and amen" to the very wise order that the Creator has established from the beginning. It is in this way that a science can constitute itself, and in particular a science which proceeds by formulating hypotheses which can be put to the test by planned experimentation.

The Crisis of Science

Some non-Christian thinkers have recognized what is essentially the umbilical cord that links the emergence of modern science to the original framework provided by a Christianized culture. They have not made note, however, of its corollary: if the God of the Bible is cast aside, the framework no longer holds together. Hence the crisis, which began several generations ago, of the ultimate end of scientific endeavor. Paradoxically, while science continues its steady march forward, its public status and the purpose of its discoveries seem adrift in a sea of uncertainty. The scholar toils away, but to what end? He finds, but what does he really discover? He no longer knows. This crisis of meaning happens to coincide with an undermining of the foundational presupposition that undergirds the entire scientific method, and that which also has made it so workable—namely, the notion that the world has a rational order and that it was fashioned by a wisdom which man was capable of apprehending. Although man belongs to that world, he stands at a sufficient remove from it, so that he might find, endowed as he is with understanding, the patterns of this creative intelligence in the world and its laws that are in operation. As soon as scholars and theorists reflecting on the scientific method refuse the idea of a Creator God—of a Moving Intelligence behind the world, having impressed on man his unique image—it becomes incomprehensible for them that the world might have a rational order and, at the same time, that man in any distinct way might be able to discover that order. There really is no reason for them to believe otherwise, if a Creator God is eliminated from the equation.

Some go so far as to say that reality has no intelligible rational order. All we can do is elaborate our hypotheses and make sure our laboratory revenues remain in the black. Along these lines is the somewhat extreme theory called "operationalism," according to which we can no longer speak of knowing reality through the scientific method. The very word "science" (which signifies "knowledge") loses its value. There remain only operations, namely those of the mathematical-technical kind. Why does something work? We have no idea! What used to pass for scientific "consensus" now amounts to nothing more than that which members of the guild see as belonging to their common self-identity myth.

Fierce debates have raged and continue to rage amongst philosophers of science with respect to the knowability of reality. Is there anything real? Does scientific theory have any connection at all with reality? Some theorists respond (and a plurality of scientific practitioners in the field follow their lead despite the ongoing crisis) that, yes, the whole of scientific methodology is constructed on the basis of this connection. Scientists must obviously probe reality through experimentation, even when it might involve roundabout ways with instruments of a complexity as imposing as those constructed at the CERN accelerator laboratory located near Geneva. They speak, revealingly, of "tracking particles," for they seek to capture something, which is another proof that man does not soliloquize when he constructs scientific theory. There is a partner in the enterprise. There is a reality which he is forced to acknowledge—it is either "yes" or "no"! Thus, the theorists are legion (including the aforementioned Karl Popper, not an inconsequential personage by any means) who maintain the connection with reality. Scientific theory is not, then, a kind of image of reality, as if it were its counterpart. It is rather a *slice* of reality, which can be compartmentalized and analyzed, and it indeed remains a slice of *reality*—hence the connection.

Others, alas, because they no longer find tenable the presupposition of faith of which we have just spoken, consider the connection inconceivable. How can reality contrive with our minds to construct hypotheses? It is better to think that everything is a projection: all comes from us, we project an order which is not really there. But such a position is *not* in accord with the scientific method, as it is normally practiced! The crisis is not resolved within the community of scholars, in any case not amongst those who truly endeavor to understand what they are doing and who continue to reflect on the underpinnings of their profession. Still, many find it more comfortable or even consider it wiser to simply "block out" questions without answers!

Scientist and Believer

Once there is an awareness of Christianity's genealogical role in the begetting and the growth of the phenomenon known as modern science, it can no longer be plausibly maintained that science is inconsistent with faith. If the Christian worldview constitutes, in a sense, the mother or the grandmother, or even the great-aunt or godmother, of science, the two cannot be held to be mutually exclusive.

The *existence of an untold number of Christian scholars*, both past and present, evangelicals or Catholics, suffices to confirm this fact. They are bona fide university professors, recognized researchers, even if they are not always the most celebrated and the most media savvy (to whom belongs the glory of this world?), who profess unequivocally their faith. They come together and mutually support one another in avowedly Christian organizations. In the past, the professor Henri Devaux, who was a member of the Institut de France, was always referenced on this score. Philippe Vernet, who was a professor at the University of Lille and one of France's elite biologists, could also be mentioned. The recently incorporated Network of Evangelical Scientists offers an excellent example of this movement. Those who suppose a priori that science and faith do not belong under the same roof might be shaken to see so many intelligent men and women, apparently in good mental health, reconcile the two so harmoniously.

Faith and Doubt

If the considerations we have just raised dispel negative attitudes with respect to science, in relating its approach to that of faith (Christian), likewise a penetrating and uncompromising analysis of faith relates its approach to that of science. Thus, self-criticism on both sides brings about a reevaluation of "received ideas." The Christian, of course, accepts whatever the supreme authority of God beckons him to believe. He knows that this entails unquestionable eternal truths. The believer, however, does not on that count consider that he knows everything! That he has laid hold of truth without needing to take any further steps forward, without lifting another finger! That the understanding he has heretofore attained is hermetically sealed, definitively and unchangeably his! For, according to the clear teaching of Scripture, the eternal truths which God shares with us in his Word are communicated through a discriminating and active *reception* on our part—or so it should be, yet it is not always the case. Let us admit that our understanding as Bible readers remains imperfect, or that it is subject to misapprehensions which compel us to make corrections and readjustments. Our minds are only too human! We are ever fallible, even while the truth that God communicates to us remains infallible, and even though the Spirit comes to help us in our weakness. Any man is a fool who would boast of having "mastered" the content of Scripture! The phrase "reformed *and* always reforming," which comes to us from the Dutch Pietists of the seventeenth century, underscores the role of self-criticism in reflecting about faith as well as about science.

By the grace granted to us, we can say that we "possess" the truth (on the assurance of 1 John 5:20), but this possession, always imperfect here below, does not give us a monopoly over the truth. It mobilizes us in the service of our beloved Savior and Lord, in so far as our thoughts align with his. It must not degenerate into an illusion of self-satisfied superiority, as if we believed ourselves uniquely inspired. On the contrary, we should remember that the storehouse of the Word is in all ways inexhaustible, that mysteries persist, that we only know in part, that there remain difficult points to be reconciled and which demand an intellectual effort always needing to be renewed. So, the dynamics of the Christian intellectual life are analogous to those of scientific endeavor.

Biblical revelation corresponds, in some sense, to the natural data which the scholar observes. The Word that God addresses to us is certain, infallible, just as the natural data that the researcher studies are his reference. He will not maintain that facts are wrong. He might be *tempted* to do so, just as we are in the Christian faith, when what the Bible teaches does not please us! If the researcher, because of the inflexibility of his hypotheses and the attachment he has for the result of his cogitations, is tempted to think that reality is wrong, he well knows that he must resist this temptation. Like the proverbial customer, reality is always right! If reality contradicts theory, it is theory that is not appropriate or sufficiently well conceived. The theory must be revised. The same applies when we must abandon our cherished biblical interpretations, in order to submit ourselves more obediently to the Word of God, in trust that his Truth is better. We act just as the scholar does when confronted with the data he studies. These data provide the standard for his scientific endeavor, as well as its coherence. In like manner, the Word of God provides the standard for our faith.

Access to Certainty

The humble acceptance of the need to probe does not preclude the assurance of convictions, both for the believer in his proper domain and for the researcher in the scientific arena. The act of faith, or the initial commitment with all the presuppositions it entails, is rationally justified by its results—by the light it sheds on the data, how it enriches understanding, and by the applications it engenders, whose usefulness shows that it is harmonious with reality. When an "act of faith" is made and only denials of reality are received in return, it can be safely assumed that a mistake has been made. But the acts of faith that lead to a richer and more satisfying reflection, as well as a more coherent and fruitful understanding of reality, are *justified*. They are not subject to the suspicion that they are arbitrary, nor born of whim or superstition. The act of faith required by scientific endeavor is justified *a posteriori* by the achievements that science engenders—whether a more coherent perspective, or the skillful classification of a multiplicity of phenomena, or the prodigious benefit that the techniques of applied science offer to humanity. Likewise, the act of faith of the believer with respect to the Bible is justified *a posteriori*. In response to the message that touches us inwardly, the act of faith is confirmed in the effects it produces. It gives rise to a new coherence, with both our vision and our experience of the world now in order and harmony.

Émile Cailliet (1894–1981), a French intellectual and Pascal specialist who made his career in the United States, once related how, in the trenches of the First World War, he had dreamed of a book that would *understand* him. Devoted professionally to understanding the masterpieces of literature, he sought such a book and could not find it, until the day his English wife, by a strange series of coincidences, brought home, where religion was never a topic of conversation, a French Bible. "I seized the book," he wrote, "and ran with it into my office. I opened it and fell on the Beatitudes! I read and read and read, and even read aloud while an indescribable warmth permeated my soul. I could find no words to express my wonder. And, suddenly, I realized, 'This is it, the book that could understand me.'"[11] The revelation of God, the inspired Scripture, is also a revelation of man. It sheds light on ourselves—and as such it is a vindication of the act of faith that we make. In the end, it is the reality with which and in which we make *meaning*. And, as in the sciences, the discovery proves its very profitability in practical application.

In theory, our survey should suffice to dispel every hesitation. To set science against faith in black and white terms, as if they were polar opposites, would be to suffer both from intellectual myopia and astigmatism. Certainly, differences which lead to contrasts can be observed. It is also quite true that the commitment required by the Christian faith is infinitely more profound, more all-encompassing, and more intimate than that required by the scholar or researcher when he "devotes" himself to his work on data (the verb "devote" tells us a lot, however, about the similarities between the two!). The scholar does not engage his entire person in the same way that the Christian is called to do. This is because of the difference in ultimate ends. The Ultimate End of Christian knowledge is the One who lays complete claim to our being and who alone has that right, He alone.

---

[11] Émile Cailliet, "The Book That Understands Me," *Christianity Today* 8, no. 4 (22 November 1963): 11.

5

RESPONSE TO THE OBJECTION

"THE FINDINGS OF SCIENTIFIC RESEARCH SHOW THE BIBLE TO BE IN ERROR, AND MOST ESPECIALLY WHEN IT COMES TO MIRACLES"

Those who are given to deep thinking are sensitive to the supposed conflict between science and belief in terms of attitudes and practices. We have attempted to show their points of convergence and the possible coordination which, on the contrary, can make of them *partners* in the investigation of reality. However, most of those who are willing to think through the issues in a responsible manner when the topic of "science and faith" comes up, with the immediate suspicion that they are opposed, look first to end results and final conclusions: the content of scientific discourse versus the content of religious discourse.

Many of those around us are persuaded that the Bible teems with stories disproven by the progress of science. They think the Bible to be only the reflection of prescientific conceptions, marked by the period in which it was written. They consider that it can no longer be taken to heart, today, without lapsing into a kind of dementia praecox, nay ridiculousness. They are convinced the Bible is filled with superstitions and infantile beliefs of a nonscientific age. For many amongst them, the belief in miracles represents the regressive naïveté of a bygone vision of the world, refuted by the discoveries of science.

We shall attempt here to entertain and examine the common objections embedded in scientific theses, in the definition and classification of phenomena, in the explanation of observable regularities (and of eventual irregularities), and in the estimations of the possible and the impossible. This assessment, intimately linked to the *predictive* function of theoretical systems, shows its greatest pertinence in the debate over miracles, which we shall treat in this final chapter.

Minor Errors Here and There?

Critics glean statements from Scripture which betray, or so they imagine, a "prescientific" misunderstanding of true causes. They pick a handful of examples, scattered throughout the Testaments, which they contrast with what is now known by "men of science." In fact, if the incidents of the supernatural are set aside (which we shall consider later), the cited cases are few and far between. The supposed difficulties resolve themselves more often than not when the author's intention in context, the literary genre, and the nuances of figurative speech are taken into account.

Let us take the noted example of the "hare that chews the cud" (Leviticus 11:6) to show how a response might be made. To try to prove that the hare in fact chews the cud (in supposing that the Hebrew, which evokes "the regurgitation of that which is half-chewed," is accurately translated) is a fine attempt, though, I believe, rather flawed. I have read authors who argue on a scientific basis that something is indeed produced in the digestive system of the hare which resembles rumination. This is possible, though it is not really germane here. Rather, we must understand the intention and the meaning of the classification in Leviticus 11.

To what, then, do we owe this classification between clean and unclean animals? It is meant to introduce a pedagogic symbolism. It is meant to inculcate in Israel the notion of pure and impure. It is for educational purposes, as the New Testament well demonstrates for the sum of provisions outside the law of Israel. While no creature of God, proceeding from him alone, is unclean in itself (Romans 14:14; 1 Timothy 4:4; cf. Mark 7:19, etc.), God instills in his people a sense of defilement (he will later reveal that true defilement is ethical and spiritual; see Mark 7 and its parallel passages) by classifying the animals into two categories, pure and impure. Human beings will belong in certain regards to the impure category (especially with reference, intriguingly, to reproduction!), and that is the point of the lesson! Since God uses here pedagogical imagery, he classifies animals according to superficial criteria, as they appear to human eyes. The texts in question in the Torah do not seek in anywise to elaborate a scientific theory, based on the "true" digestive system of any animal. As parents illustrate adult notions for children, the Lord simplifies with first appearances, so he can get his point across. It matters little whether the creature in question is a true or false ruminant according to the criteria of contemporary animal physiology. To accuse the biblical text of scientific error in this regard is to be grossly mistaken. It is to be blind to the obvious meaning!

Some charge the psalmist with advancing the "astrological" notion that the moon causes illnesses (Psalm 121:6). It takes a twisted mind to draw such a sure conclusion in this sense from a fragment of poetry which is moreover phrased only negatively: the moon will not harm you. . . . The promise runs parallel to that of the sun, whose "scorching" effects are felt without reference to folklore beliefs. The same kind of response can be made to those who find traces of "superstition" in Psalm 58:5–6 when it evokes the art of serpent charmers—wholly ineffectual, by the way! Calvin long ago, in his *Commentary on the Psalms*, resolved this difficulty. He reminds those of us who take the revealed writings seriously that magic spells can exert an influence, and are on that account proscribed. They have an impact not because they have any real power in themselves, quite obviously, but rather "by a pure sleight of Satan." Calvin wisely points out, ever the skilled philologist that he is, that David borrows his imagery here from the popular view of serpents to denounce the venomous calumnies of the wicked. To draw theoretic conclusions about the efficacy of enchantments is to lack, quite sadly, any exegetical astuteness.

Others question Jacob's "scheming" when he seems to have recourse to sympathetic magic in placing branches with peeled white stripes in front of flocks in heat so that they might bear streaked young (Genesis 30:27–42). And it worked! We now know, however, that whatever advantageous effect came about for the clever patriarch resulted from the application of Mendel's laws concerning the heredity of genetic characteristics, which Jacob could not have suspected. I accept this verdict concerning the incident. Nevertheless, I note that the inspired text *says nothing* about the mechanisms in play. It in no way validates the thoughts that might be supposed in the mind of Jacob. As this passage evinces, the Bible does not depict individuals as infallible, nor does it extend the divine blessing to the wholesale approval of their viewpoints and actions.

In this first category of objections raised against faith in Science's name, I can find none truly capable of unsettling belief.

The Structure of Reality

The objections relative to *cosmology*—to the image that we make of the fundamental components and structures of the reality we experience—are legion. The rift between modern science and the worldview attested by the Bible, reckon the critics, opens a yawning chasm. On the one hand, biblical cosmology is typically seen harkening back to *the age of myth*. On the other, Christian faith adds an *invisible dimension* that it is not considered scientific to admit.

It is repeated to us ad nauseam that, for the Hebrews, the earth is flat and rests on pillars that plunge into the great abyss. Above them extends a firmament, considered a solid vault, without which the waters would cascade onto the earth and bring about a tremendous catastrophe. This firmament must be solid, for the waters which it retains form a celestial ocean. When it rains, it is due to apertures in the firmament through which the liquid falls. Such is, so they maintain, the conception of the world that the Hebrews had, and which finds itself expressed in numerous passages in the Old Testament. Of course, it is no longer admissible for us to accept such a cosmology! In the New Testament, as they further maintain, another conception of the world is found, in three stages: the subterranean world, the earth, and the heavenly realms (see Philippians 2:10, "in heaven and on earth and under the earth" [ESV]). A conception of this sort is deemed mythological. The German theologian Rudolf Bultmann made a name for himself as the trailblazer of his generation in calling for the "demythologization" of the New Testament. He insisted that this worldview, which is no longer our own, shaped the apostolic message. One of the chief conceptions it includes, unacceptable for modern man, is the belief, which we shall treat anon, in the existence of *spirits*, of invisible and powerful agents capable of interfering in the phenomena of this world. That spirits could produce real effects in daily life and in nature itself was, of course, what everyone believed at the time, but it is a mode of thinking which science now enjoins us forevermore to repudiate!

Galileo's trial in the seventeenth century often serves as a convenient reference point for those who oppose science and faith to each other. Galileo was condemned by the Inquisition because he taught that the earth revolved around the sun, and not vice versa. His teaching appeared incompatible with that of certain biblical passages (the sun seems to rise, fall). His trial is cited as proof positive of an inevitable conflict: when people of faith wish to remain faithful to the biblical text, they cannot help but condemn the findings of modern science. Modern science, in return, retraces its veritable beginnings to Galileo, and the Inquisition well understood the threat. Some historians, it is true, have argued that Galileo's trial issued from a much more complex set of factors: it was not only his views on cosmology which were called into question, but his trial served to his benefit as the means of dissimulating even graver suspicions. According to this hypothesis, the pope, who was Galileo's protector, knew that he was going to be accused of heresies considered far more dangerous than the cosmological thesis (theses that could have impacted Eucharistic dogma), and would have sought to shield him by refocusing the trail on the question of the earth's rotation. We have perhaps not yet heard the last word on the story. Galileo's trial has nevertheless remained a potent symbol. To evoke Galileo is tantamount to saying: "Remember the wrong the Christian church brought upon herself by attaching herself too closely to the teachings of Scripture. Science and faith must thus be kept entirely separate." For freethinkers, this unfortunate seventeenth-century episode has resulted in the pure and simple condemnation of faith.

What might be the response? On the issue of cosmology, the conflict is in large part nonexistent, for the image of the world commonly attributed to Scripture is in reality quite foreign to it. With respect to the cosmology commonly taught by the sciences, I can see no particular problem. It has a high degree of plausibility. Rather, it is the cosmological theory attributed to the Bible that is not plausible! Lyric texts, in which mention is made of the pillars of the earth and of the floodgates of the heavens, are taken out of context and their poetic quality is entirely overlooked! Extrapolating from there, it is imagined that such is what truly "the Hebrews believed." Images appearing in poetic texts are even incompatible amongst themselves if taken literally, instead of treating them as the figures of speech they should be. Here pillars are described, there it would appear the sky is a solid vault, and still in another place the sky is a soft fabric that the Lord spreads out like the canvas of a tent (Isaiah 40:22). The fact that so many different images can be employed shows that there is no *single* theory that the biblical authors ascribed to, as taught with divine sanction, concerning the structure of the cosmos and the seeming firmness of the celestial vault. It has been maintained that the word used in Genesis 1 and often translated as "expanse" (v. 6) or "firmament" implies a solid dome. We are told that for the Hebrews, the sky consisted of a solid sphere. The solidity of this arch kept the celestial ocean, lodged above, from crashing down onto the earth in a deadly flood. The Hebrew word itself (*raqiya'*) does not even signify "solid vault." The term comes from metallurgy, it is true, but it evokes a sheet of metal (of gold, for example) beat extremely thin. Such a sheet could be extremely light, and it is hammered so as to give it the greatest extension possible, hence the translation "expanse." To conclude from this sole use of the term in the Bible that the Hebrews believed in a solid celestial vault is intellectually irresponsible. As for the "floodgates of the heavens," Psalm 78 clearly shows that the Hebrews did not have in mind the image of an arch with pierced windows. Verse 23 contains a synonymic parallelism, classic in Hebraic poetry: "Yet he commanded the skies above and opened the doors of heaven" (ESV). The psalmist is speaking here of the clouds. He must not ignore the fact that the rain comes from the clouds (as the preceding Psalm, 77:18, clearly evinces), and he could have read in the book of Job the specific mention of the processes of evaporation and of condensation as the origin of rain (Job 36:27–28). If he employs the expression "open the doors of heaven" for the onset of the rain, it is because he expects more astuteness on the part of his readers than found amongst our contemporaries, often too obtuse to grasp the poetry. To attribute to the biblical authors a ridiculous cosmology from a modern standpoint issues from a *misunderstanding* which seems to owe a lot to the *disdain* that so-called "scientists" have for nonscientists.

What strikes us when we read the Scriptures and compare them with the sacred writings of the surrounding cultures of the same period is not so much their anticipation of modern science—which is rarely the case—but that they show themselves to be *cautious* in this regard, nay I would almost say "chaste." However serendipitously, the Bible avoids making pronouncements that would reflect the opinions of the time and which today would be completely unacceptable. The Bible tends to opt for a poetic style, or to evoke first appearances, as the eye immediately sees (a language said to be *phenomenological*). There is nothing untoward in describing biblical language in these terms. The Bible does not propose a theory for the specific mechanisms behind the phenomena it describes. It thus avoids linking itself to the pseudoscientific theory of a bygone era, now untenable. It is rather remarkable to observe how the Bible has succeeded in preserving itself from the contamination of the cosmological beliefs of its time. We only find a poetic echo of them. They are not presented as elements of an elaborated theory of the world. This fact seems significant.

Some go further still and deem it nonscientific to speak of a soul that would be distinct from the body. "I can find no soul under my scalpel." This materialist refusal extends to all that is unseen—at the same time "the world beyond" involving the present existence "somewhere" of the souls and spirits of deceased humans and the entire host of invisible entities such as angels or demons (and also djinns, gnomes, etc.), which holds so much sway in the popular piety of all religions. Scriptural teaching on this subject is swept away along with the whole hodgepodge of vain imaginations. It offers even the privileged example of these fanciful "worlds beyond worlds" upon which Nietzsche heaped his sarcasms.

It must be observed that a de facto alliance exists between the vogue of science in our recent Western culture and materialism as the dominant philosophy for a very large part of the population. However, we have no cause to let ourselves be intimidated, and *with good reason*. The materialist option does not derive from any science worthy of the name, but from philosophic or ideological preferences. The proof of this, once again, is the number of prestigious scholars—not only found in ancient history, but present-day—who do not share this assessment, who dare to contradict it. If the fruits of scientific research compelled every right and sober mind to deny the soul and the invisible, these scholars would constitute a monstrous anomaly. This is not so. A Nobel Prize winner such as Sir John Eccles, for example, vigorously maintains the *double* composition of human beings. The invisible, by definition, is not evident to the senses, and therefore cannot be demonstrated by the ordinary testing processes that weigh and measure. To deny the spiritual realm out of hand is only begging the question. Experience itself sometimes renders it "palpable." I once recall a pastor (the German pastor-theologian Otto Rodenberg), trained in the demythologizing school and persuaded that demons were only superstitious chimeras, forced to yield to the evidence in his first parish call—evidence of a demonization and the deliverance thereof in the name of Jesus.

We shall concede this point: the researcher's self-imposed discipline does not dispose him to acknowledge the invisible. He is justifiably focused on natural causalities and cannot take into account the possible interferences of ephemeral spiritual entities. He is trained to always verify before affirming. As for human subjects, the "psychosomatic" union of the soul and body makes it difficult for him to imagine a soul existing without a body, with another status than that of its bodily function. Nothing, however, compels any *denial*. It is through a pure power grab—illegitimate, to be sure—that the scholar decrees the nonexistence of all that eludes the implements of his method. Conversely, the scholar must suffer from a strange blind spot not to see that science itself is not intelligible if thought is *reduced* to the corporeal. The freedom to form diverse hypotheses and to probe their *veracity*! The marvelous connivance between independent reality and the workings of human intelligence! (Let us remember Einstein: "The most incomprehensible thing about the world is that it is comprehensible.") None of this easily inserts itself into the materialist framework. The strength of Pascal's reflection remains entire: "Out of all bodies together we could not succeed in creating one little thought. It is impossible, and of a different order" (*Pensées*, 793 according to Brunschvicg, 308 according to Lafuma). Except for those who hold an antispiritual bias, the analysis of the conditions of knowledge favor the affirmation of the spirit, distinct from the body.

Science and Faith in Relation to Origins

For the general public, the field of *cosmogony* constitutes without doubt the most well-known battleground between science and faith, due to certain politicized and highly publicized debates across the Atlantic—debates (not to mention trials) which bring into direct confrontation expert proponents of the "official" line versus radical antievolutionists. The latter define themselves as "creationists" and militate in the name of the Bible. The conflict comes to a head in the discourse each side has adopted, involving the synthesis of findings purportedly averred by research. Cosmogony, to be distinguished from cosmology, concerns the origins of the material world, including those of life and humankind (*Homo sapiens*). It merits, in our rapid survey here, a special treatment,[12] for the question concerning the genesis of the cosmos and of humankind is complex. Finding themselves commonly added to the mix are questions of a quite different order: how the future is comprehensively viewed, for its schema plays the role of a heuristic principle (i.e., it orients and guides research); how observed data are dealt with, whether in fossil form or in the present state of nature; how hypotheses are more or less plausibly made to link these data together and to reconstitute the mechanisms of diversification; and how to conduct proper exegesis of scriptural texts, taking into account the reach claimed by their authority and their literary genres. On these topics, I have surveyed in rather great detail what I believe relevant in my book *In the Beginning: The Opening Chapters of Genesis.* Although the scientific information in my earlier study might be updated, my proposed conclusions remain the same and, for the sake of brevity here, I refer the reader to its pages. For a more recent treatment, I am only too glad to refer the reader to the works of Lydia Jaeger or those published under her direction (in whose number I am honored to be counted). Her skill set does not lack any tool: having at once competencies as a trained physicist, a philosopher of science, and an insightful and rigorous theologian.

As is not uncommon in disputes, both sides share some of the blame. Not a few who have taken it upon themselves to speak in the name of science, seeking to discredit the Christian belief in a Creator, have overplayed their hand. They neglect to question themselves. They extrapolate with excessive audacity. They fall into ideology. In brief, they would do well to be more modest. As

---

[12] Cf. Lydia Jaeger's recent study, *Adam, qui es-tu? Perspectives bibliques et scientifiques sur l'origine de l'humanité* (Charols/Paris: Excelsis/Groupes Bibliques Universitaires, 2013).

for the defenders of the Bible, falling into their own excess, they attribute to the Word of God what is not always found in Scripture. If some make science say more than it does, it so happens as well that some make Scripture say more than it does—when it is not understood in context, when figurative language is not taken into account, when methods of rigorous interpretation are not applied. In general, antagonisms result from one or the other of these distortions or unfounded misrepresentations, if not both at the same time.

The prevailing thesis in scientific circles explains the genealogical diversification of living species and often the development of all things since the initial *big bang* by the processes of *evolution*. If the proposed datings are accepted—and the procedures implemented for determining these harmonize remarkably well—our universe, such as we know it, began about 13.4 billion years ago (for a long time atheist scholars resisted tooth and nail the notion of a beginning, which for them brought creation too much to mind, and although many still seek to circumvent the matter, it remains today the viewpoint of almost all specialists). Once life appeared, the series of fossils that have been discovered suggests, by their chronological breakdown, a "familial" continuity among life forms, the most recent "descending" from the preceding, and their modifications engendering the diversity of species. This is evolution in the strictest sense. Charles Darwin conceived the basic mechanism of its progress, which accredited scientists still retain—the combination of *changes* due to chance (Darwin was unaware of the laws of heredity, later included in the theory, and genetic mutations due to chance) and of *natural selection*.

To reconstruct the past, scientists seek to connect the dotted lines between established facts, and every hypothesis lays itself open to possible criticism. It is characteristic of the scientific spirit to encourage this criticism! Since Darwin, dissenting scientists have critiqued, in the name of science, the scenario accepted by majority opinion. That Darwinian theory has been able to resist so long and that it has been able to enrich itself with a brand-new discipline, molecular biology, increases somewhat its plausibility.

Its principal weakness, without being removed, tends to lessen. The Darwinian mechanism still seems incapable mathematically of explaining evolution in the proposed time frame (pure chance would have required billions of years more than the age of the universe), but corollary mechanisms have been discovered which have reduced the gap in the calculations and the phenomena—phenomena which must, according to the classic expression, be "recovered." The credibility of the theory has somewhat been reinforced over the course of recent decades.

In any event, the success of Neo-Darwinism continues on three fronts. It applies to the emergence of humanity to which we all belong: this development, in itself, is hardly surprising for those who adopt evolutionist perspectives concerning the origin of species—except a sustained effort can be observed to minimize the difference between "modern" *homo sapiens* and the "men" or hominids that preceded him, along with the whole animal kingdom. The advocates of such a reductionism believe they are simply compensating for the "nonscientific" separation which religions have too long established between man and animals. We need not have our antennae up to detect here an admixture of ideological aggressiveness. Research in ethology contributes to rendering porous the definitional borders of humanness. The second front which can be observed concerns the history of *homo sapiens* whose "life course" is interpreted according to the interplay of chance and of natural selection. It might be wondered whether we are not in the presence here of an excessive biologization of history, which would eclipse its other categories and would obscure its meaning as *driven* by free agents—in the final analysis by the Sovereign Agent. In the third place, the intellectual satisfaction which evolutionism brings, in the awareness of the multiplicity of life and of its prodigious adaptations, accustoms the mind to consider everything from the angle of change. The modern worldview is *genetic*. A thing is what it is because of what it has *become*. For some, the full import of this perspective goes to the point of making Evolution the universal key of all meaning, able to answer ultimate questions. We can perceive here the makings of a quasi-religious commitment. Evolution becomes the Dogma from which the slightest deviation elicits pious protestations: Heresy! Blasphemy!

In the minds of many nonbelieving scientists as well as a "right" wing of conservative evangelicalism, the evolutionist thesis, at whatever level, is totally opposed to the teaching of the Bible, and in particular to the witness of the first chapters of the book of Genesis. In general, both camps read these chapters as if they taught that the world was created but a few thousand years ago, in seven days of a duration like our present days, so that the incompatibility between the two accounts of life's origins is assumed to be entire. I trust that I have shown that this reading of the creation narrative, which has occasioned the seeming insoluble problem, is devoid of justification. Ironically, for certain believers, in their intense desire to remain faithful to the biblical text, this reading is actually *unfaithful* to the biblical text. It ignores several data, it misses the central point—what the biblical text really seeks to signify, according to the intention of the human author, according to the intention of the Spirit that led him. For whoever examines the biblical narratives with sufficient knowledge of the original languages and of the modes of expression of their time (including the choice of their literary genre and of their eventual reediting), for whoever makes due allowance for the insertion of an explanatory clause such as the one found in Genesis 2:5 "for the LORD God had not sent rain on the earth" (NIV), for whoever familiarizes himself with word study and the theological connotations of imagery, for whoever takes into account future references in the Holy Scriptures, the *literalist* bias shows itself to be inadequate. The serious analysis of the biblical texts leads to a well-founded conclusion: they do not intend to furnish us with the *date* of origins, and are compatible with the use by God of *evolutionary* procedures for his work of creation. In this respect, the conflict that was imagined with the prevailing scientific discourse is reversed.

All is not resolved, however. In all fairness, it is permitted to find the tone of certain scholars to be too dogmatic. Even considering alone the evolutionist account of the diversity of species, to deny the hypothetical aspect of the theory is to gloss over the uncertainties that remain (in spite of all the progress made) with respect to the mechanisms at play. This is also to make light of the difficulty of reconstructing the remote past, based on patchy evidence. It is to ignore the "epistemological" status (i.e., the philosophic dimension of the sciences) of a concept such as evolution, so totalizing that it furnishes a hypermodel justified by its usefulness, by the intelligibility it engenders, but is incapable of being formally evidenced in a laboratory. When Evolution becomes the key to the meaning of existence, and when every criticism leveled at it is considered blasphemous, evolutionist ideology *usurps* the proper role accorded to science. It is transformed into a quasi-sect and makes itself the rival of biblical religion. No compromise, no concession. The conflict then surpasses that of a simple opposition between scientific theory and faith. It becomes an idolatry that absolutizes a certain aspect of reality. We would say, however, that the evolution of species can belong to reality even while its absolutization merits resistance.

Concerning *human* origins, a subject that is not without importance to faith, I shall not gainsay the tension that exists. Between the biblical material, conscientiously interpreted with the aid of available resources, and the findings of scientific research—subject to review, of course—the gulf is wide. Yet there is no reason to panic. A distinction must first be made: the emergence of *Adamic* humanity, "created in the image of God," that by preference I term *homo theologus* or *theologicus*, does not coincide necessarily with that of the forms described in scientific theory. In any case, *homo erectus* does not yet belong to that particular category, neither does *homo neanderthalensis*. The spiritual dimension, with the vocation of communing with the Creator, can correspond to a threshold impossible to discern in the fossils. The dossier concerning the advancement constituted by conscientious reflection, the development of complex languages, and culture which changes the face of the world, is weighty. Only reductionists minimize the factual data. It would not appear impossible to interpret Genesis 4 (which plays a certain role in the debate) in a nonliteral fashion. I believe, however, that it is necessary to maintain an individual Adam as the ancestor of all our common humanity, and thus to resist the temptation to eliminate this biblical datum which for the moment paleo-anthropology does not endorse. It is not detrimental, in spite of its discomfort, that an unresolved difficulty checks our all-too-natural desire for security and command, that it obliges us to trust—trust in the pure truth of the revealed Word, trust in the fitful progress of scientific research kept from straying too long and too far from "common grace."

The Question of Miracles

The particular question of *miracles* is another arena of combat. For many, to believe in miracles is ipso facto to oppose science. We can distinguish two principal forms this incompatibility takes.

For one school of thought, science entails a thoroughgoing determinism. All the events that take place in reality are embedded in a network of cause and effect, governed by laws that do not allow the slightest exception: everything is determined by the laws of nature. Since miracles are understood as interrupting, suspending, or violating their operation, they are deemed utterly unfeasible. The scientific view of the world is that of a circle (entirely closed) of cause and effect, and the miraculous is treated as if it were an unthinkable breach. There can be no tearing in the unified cloth which is nature—whose laws the academic has formulated as warp and weft! It is well-nigh impossible for him to admit the miraculous if he wants to remain in good scientific standing.

Others advocate a softer and subtler approach. They acknowledge this determinism cannot be averred. It is a philosophic position that extends beyond the scope of what a scholar can stipulate. It is actually rather the case that some scientific theories of the twentieth century point to a certain indeterminism. Since they cannot ascribe to a complete determination of all events in a closed system of causes and consequences, the miraculous cannot be excluded in this way. What they prefer to say then is that a scientific *attitude* consists in seeking out rational causes and in establishing causal sequences according to established laws, to which a mathematical form has generally been given. He who believes in miracles adopts, in his relationship with the phenomenon, a nonscientific *attitude*. A scholar worthy of the name of scholar does not have this right to consider miracles, if he wants to remain in his guild and continue to merit the credit that this status grants him. He must seek another explanation, he must seek the laws at work. The postulate of the scientific method expels from its field of investigation every phenomenon that would lie outside of causal networks. In essence, although absolute determinism might no longer be affirmed a priori in order to discount the miraculous, the softer and subtler approach amounts to much the same thing. For all intents and purposes, miracles are proscribed. He who accepts the miraculous condemns himself from the start for adopting a nonscientific approach, for deviating from the right mental framework.

If it were rationally advanced that other pathways of knowledge exist, having their own inner consistency, than only the modern conception of science, it might not do us any good. Such voices are rarely raised, and remain practically inaudible when they do. The connotation "nonscientific" is commonly treated as "irresponsible." All the ponderousness and all the prestige that are associated with the word "scientist" serve to belittle the "nonscientific" attitude of those who are willing to entertain the possibility of miracles. Thus, the Nobel Prize winner Jacques Monod could say, with respect to cosmogony, that the scientific attitude implies that seeking any design in nature must be renounced. A design supposes a conscious agent who has a purpose (on this point, the Nobel Prize winner was perspicacious). The scientific attitude is limited to seeking efficient causes, and should never consider purposes. The person who believes he sees a miracle thereby discerns a thought or a design behind the phenomenon. This stance places him at the opposite pole of scientific endeavor—implying as well that he stands at the opposite pole of rightly ordered reason.

Whether miracles are categorically denied for transgressing the laws of nature and breaching the cause-effect relationship, assuming such things never occur, or whether belief in miracles is condemned as belonging to an aberrant mental attitude, the supernatural no longer has any place in the worldview of a self-respecting scientist in the twenty-first century.

The Objection to Miracles

Many unbelievers around us hold to the facile solution: they do not believe miracles occur. They remain attached to their *scientism*, which is a sort of "religion of science" typical of the latter half of the nineteenth century and which has not disappeared in our times. A handful of theologians—hardly evangelical—concerned to appear modern and to obtain a favorable hearing in the present age, have said much the same thing. In a lecture titled "New Testament and Mythology," Rudolf Bultmann, a German theologian of the New Testament who dominated the theology of Protestant churches in the 1940s and 1950s (and whose influence is still felt), affirms quite clearly that to imagine the circle of laws and effects at some time interrupted by a divine power is to adopt a mythological view of the world which modern man can no longer accept. Those who do so evince a sort of schizophrenia, a dichotomy of the mind, a kind of intellectual double standard whose dupes they have become.

Those who do not go as far, and who cautiously question non-scientific attitudes and methods, do not seem conscious of their own inconsistency. I have in mind here other theologians, professing Christians. They first appear to admit other realms of knowledge than the scientific, but doing a double take, they act as if the scientific approach were the only right one, legitimate and responsible for a rational spirit of today.

Their stance takes on a sharper edge in a famous fallback argument, which undermines all belief in miracles attested throughout history, such as those which have been believed on the authority of ancient witnesses. The Scottish philosopher David Hume, in the eighteenth century, came up with the new line of reasoning. It is based on the hard-to-dispute notion that "the historian must weigh probabilities." He considers the witnesses and must determine, each time, whether the probabilities favoring the testimony carry the day or on the contrary whether the probabilities are less favorable. In the case of a "miracle testimony," it must be admitted that the chances that a miracle took place are very weak (otherwise it would not be a miracle). The probabilities of a miracle hold little sway in view of the greater likelihood that the witness lied, was tricked, or had hallucinations. Given this unequal measure, it can be said that the chances that the testimony lacks consistency are always weightier. The scientific method, throughout history, is thus always going to reject the testimony of miracles. A good historian, who desires to be seen as rational and scientific, must always conclude: "So, a miracle is said to have taken place? I must consider that the witness probably lied or was tricked, rather than give credence to the reality of a miraculous act or event." Hume applies this reasoning most especially to the resurrection of Jesus Christ, which, while belonging to the category of the miraculous, represents much more than a miracle, for it is the very keystone event of all Christianity.

Some would add to this indictment against the notion of miracles and against the notion that these might serve to confirm the Christian faith that "miracles" exist everywhere, in all religions and in all sects. Almost every organized devotion in the history of humanity appeals to miracles. And there are some doozies! Some religious enthusiasts are healed by bathing in the Gange, just as they would be in making a pilgrimage to Lourdes, or in Pentecostal gatherings. What is the value of these duly attested incidents as confirmatory signs of true doctrine?

When such miracles are analyzed, it becomes apparent that they are poorly explained phenomena, but for which it must be said collective psychology plays a very important role. If throngs are prepared to expect wonders, they end up seeing wonders. The news is then bruited about, it spreads, it becomes magnified. The chain reaction of such phenomena is commonly observed. People crave tales of the miraculous. As soon as some sensational stories are related in the pulpit, even in a traditional church, it immediately captivates attention! People are so desperate for miracles to occur, almost wishing to reduce them to a formula like a law of social psychology, that in the context of intense collective desire, the rumor is easily conceived—

and grows—which reports that the thing actually took place. This is what the study of rumors teaches. The appetite for wonders is such that stories of miracles are elaborated and embellished. It cannot be considered that reports of this type hold any sway.

Lastly, and we arrive here at the most sophisticated level of the indictment, some critics say they would be prepared to believe in God through a *purer* form of faith, which has no need of miracles. For them, the idea of God—Being itself, the Absolute and Infinite, ultimate Wisdom and Good—is not only noble, but necessary for minds with a metaphysical bent, yet the concept of the miraculous upsets this view. How could a God have so poorly calculated his actions that he would be obliged, from time to time, to *improvise* and to "rectify" them? Psalm 148 declares that God has established the heavens and the earth once for all and in perpetuity, that he gave them laws "which shall not pass" (v. 6 KJV)! Miracles would then be a violation of the laws established by God! For these critics, a God who abstains from such improvisations, from such irregularities, and who does not indulge the great unwashed in their unwholesome interest in the extraordinary, is much worthier of admiration and adoration!

How can we counter such an insidious indictment?

The Case for Miracles

The response might be made along two basic lines. The first would show that the understanding of miracles that the objectors have in mind is not entirely accurate. While it is not totally foreign to the biblical notion of the miraculous, it does not correspond either to its dominant strains. There is at least here a correction to bring to bear. The second line will contest the scientistic conception of the world which undergirds false notions about miracles.

The Biblical Conception of Miracles

1. The first point to underscore is that the idea of violation of the laws of nature is not at the forefront of the scriptural narrative

when miracles are treated. It might be wondered whether this is strictly speaking a biblical notion—especially when terms as loaded as "transgression" and "violation" are employed. Many phenomena called miracles in Scripture took place according to causal chain reactions, in an entirely ordinary manner, which did not bring about any apparent transgression of the normal workings of the cosmos. It is mainly through the interpretation which several evangelical commentators have given to miracles which, on the surface and perhaps due to the heritage of Sunday school, seem to be transgressions of the laws of nature. If the language of the Bible is better understood, however, this is not the case.

Let us consider, for example, the famous episode of the sun that Joshua would have caused to stand still—implying that the entire solar system had paused for a few hours, entailing the abrogation of all the laws of gravitation. Is that what the text really says? It does not appear so. An evangelical scholar and expert in ancient languages (professor at the Princeton School of Theology), Robert Dick Wilson, was able to demonstrate by citing Mesopotamian astronomical tables that the biblical language signifies that, in reality, an eclipse took place. God so ordered this natural phenomenon to occur at that precise moment, thus throwing confusion into the enemy ranks and permitting Joshua to seize the victory. The miracle was the coincidence, in God's plan, between the battle and the eclipse (which informed astronomers would have predicted, with its exact time).

Concerning the crossing of the Sea of Reeds (*yam sûf*, and not the Red Sea—later texts speak of the Red Sea but the text in Exodus, Exodus 14, speaks of the Sea of Reeds), often the phenomenon is imagined whereby all the laws of nature were violated, where the waters, all of a sudden, stood vertical, forming an aquatic wall as if frozen (with salt water no less!). The language of Exodus and the references made later to the episode can be interpreted in an entirely different sense. The waters formed a rampart, a wall, but not in the literal sense of a straight-cut panel. They formed a rampart with *respect to the Egyptians*, who were on the attack (as is evidenced by the translation "fortified wall" in Exodus 14:22 and Psalm 78:13). It is probable that, in a marshy area of a depth of one or two meters, with systems of small lakes interconnected by narrow passageways, an extremely powerful wind drove and backed up a mass of water of one of the swampy lakes to another, making a dry passage. The waters thus piled up formed a kind of rampart, which permitted the children of Israel to pass through. Then, when the Egyptians threw themselves headlong after the Israelites (would they have done so if they had seen a wall of water ten meters high?), God changed the direction of the wind, and the piled-up waters gushed down upon them. This is likely what happened. It is a plausible interpretation of the biblical texts, which remains faithful to them. Here again, no particular transgression of the laws of nature occurred, but only a synchronization in conformity with the Lord's plan.

2. The principal *biblical terms* for speaking of the miracles do not imply per se that there is a discontinuity in the causal chain, or transgression of the laws of nature. The three terms employed (all present in Hebrews 2:4) are "signs," "wonders," and "miracles." The word "miracle" is literally "power." It connotes a phenomenon which discharges a great store of energy. The power manifests itself in the event taking place. It can be something which causes phenomena to coincide. It does not necessarily violate the laws of nature. The second term "wonder" implies something extraordinary. It designates the unusual and draws attention for this reason. The Greek word *téras* (genitive, *tératos*) is used as a root in French— hence one speaks of "tératologie" for the study of monstrosities. That which is monstrous is unusual. The work of wonder stuns, astonishes, but here again, there is no particular insistence on the laws of nature being violated. The third term is the richest in meaning, since it signifies "sign." The Gospel of John uses only this term to speak of the miracles of Jesus. Emphasis is laid on the message which the miracle, symbolically, must impress on those who are its witnesses. In biblical terminology, miracles are signs conveying and concentrating meaning, but which must be discerned and rightly understood.

The terms in the Old Testament do not correspond strictly speaking to the three terms found in the New Testament. The principal word corresponds precisely to "signs" (in Hebrew *'ōt*), and can be employed for signs that have nothing to do with the miraculous, just like the Greek word in the New Testament. It is the term employed for announcing the miracle of the Virgin Birth of the Messiah in Isaiah 7. But God also gives for a "sign" to his messenger Moses the specific prediction that the people of Israel "shall worship God on this mountain" (Exodus 3:12 NRSV). This is not expressly a miracle; it is a point of reference which will permit Moses to attach his faith to something tangible. Another word is translated "wonder" in several versions. It, too, connotes the conveyance of meaning. Another term has a broader usage and evokes that which goes beyond the capacities of human beings, which differentiates the heavenly and the earthly: "marvels." None of these terms lays emphasis on the violation of the laws of nature, but rather on a series of traits: something highly unusual which surprises, which displays a power that is not at the disposal of man. Something humans only dream about without ever being able to carry out on their own now *takes place*! Whether improbable coincidences that occur at just the right moment or certain unhoped-for expectations that are fulfilled! It is the power of God that is thereby denoted. This power does not act simply to be seen. Rather, it is designed to challenge, to instruct, and always to reveal the presence of God. The biblical perspective on miracles beckons first and foremost to show interest in their meaning.

For all the biblical writers, miracles are conceived of as divine interventions in *a system where God is active and directs everything* that takes place. Miracles are unusual, it goes without saying. However, at bottom, they do not differ from other events which occur, since everything proceeds from God. God directs everything that happens according to the counsel of his will (Ephesians 1:11). It has been stated, a bit tongue in cheek, that it should be not said that "it rains," but rather that "God rains," or more precisely, that "God makes it rain." Everything that takes place issues from the activity of the Most High who superintends all things and who orders all things with wisdom. Miracles belong to the workings of God. An ancient expression for them is most apropos: they are "extraordinary providences." God governs all things and provides for the needs of his creatures, sustaining them. Without him, everything would collapse, as Psalm 104 states. God acts in his providence, in a regulated and usual manner. However, he dispenses freely *as well* certain "extraordinary providences." Thus, God intervenes, provides in another manner, according to need, while drawing ever more attention to his superintending and redemptive work. In sum, in response to ill-informed objections, it must be emphasized: in the biblical worldview, miracles are integrated into a larger whole which might simply be called divine providence.

The Response to Scientism

Once this has been clearly understood, we are primed to take on scientism. The concept of a causality closed in on itself, of a circle of laws impossible to break, is, on the one hand, a philosophic position among others, in no wise necessary to scientific endeavor. On the other hand, it is in contradiction with the biblical vision of reality. This biblical vision, let us recall, has served as a basis for the flourishing of modern science, and it is completely compatible with the development of the sciences.

On what grounds is it postulated, because a certain number of regular correlations in the world have been found, that a *closed* circle is therefore constituted? No, it is a kind of decree, a philosophic *ukase* that corresponds to scientism and not to science. Not only is it arbitrary, but it entraps those submitted to it in a situation from which they cannot escape, and which is full of despair. They are forever blocked in an impasse. For henceforth, what do we make of man? What do we make of the freedom that scientists themselves deploy when they build their scientific systems? How can they truly act, if everything is determined in a circle of causes and effects? Some thinkers have admitted the tough pill to swallow, with a bitter aftertaste in their mouths. Freedom is only an illusion, for ultimate reality only amounts to a clash of atoms, only these laws of physics are in operation, behavior is only an effect due to causes of which the individual is not conscious. How can these thinkers even make such statements with any intellectual consistency? Unless they consider freedom to be autonomous, to be outside the circle? It is quite difficult to deny the intimate experience of freedom. The problem in trying to make freedom coexist with a determinism closed in on itself is ultimately insolvable, philosophically, for those who adopt the scientistic position.

The adepts of scientism are fewer and farther between today than they were in the nineteenth century, in particular because of the evolution of thought on the part of scholars themselves. Many are prepared to say that they no longer quite know what the notion of causality relates to. What we observe are correlations. We draw out of them equations, but what does that mean? . . . Scholars themselves are sometimes highly skeptical. The biblical notion of laws established by God for the proper functioning of nature corresponds much better to the newfound modesty of scholars of our times when they try to define the laws they have formulated and put them into equations. For many, these laws are just observable patterns of particles or of elements of nature, about which it can be said that at least statistically there are X number of chances for one thing to occur and another not . . . and this approaches somewhat the biblical conception! The Lord God has arranged the natural world with an order, he has established regular correlations, but he has not thereby tied his own hands! His is not a system that would stand on its own and remain closed in on itself. The correlations and operating rules are at the disposal of the Lord and need him to exist. There therefore remains nothing in scientism to intimidate us, if we strip it of its false prestige, if we resist the intellectual overconfidence of some of its defenders. Theirs is not a very strong position!

The biblical position is thoroughly compatible with science. Given that God established certain regularities, the researcher can examine them, carry out experiments with a view to unlocking their mechanisms, repeat them in the laboratory, and finally quantify them. That does not exclude God from acting, too, if he so pleases, outside of these regularities.

We are obliged to affirm that God does this very thing, that he acts outside of these regularities which scholars call the "laws of nature." We have given several examples of biblical miracles in which that has perhaps not taken place, as some suppose. In certain cases, however, we must simply admit that God acts outside these laws. He does not constrain himself to the ordinary correlations. When Elisha came to the aid of a companion who had lost an ax-head at the bottom of a body of water (he had borrowed the ax and in that day it was very costly!), and when the prophet caused it to float to the surface, it was an action well out of the ordinary. How did God accomplish this? He did not cancel the laws of gravity, but he caused, in this open system which is at his disposal, another force to bring it to the surface. Out of the ordinary! When Daniel's three companions were thrown into the fiery furnace and remained perfectly preserved, it cannot be said to be a natural occurrence. It cannot be a simple coincidence between causal chains as in the exodus. Once again, it was a phenomenon "out of the ordinary." God intervened in a special way. If the system of causes and effects is open, nothing inhibits God from intervening. It is an opening which permits as well our freedom to intervene between causes and effects, a freedom moved by God, according to his infinitely wise and mysterious manner of working. Our freedom introduces thus new causalities into the fabric which constitutes nature.

The Yearning for Miracles

What can be said about the "yearning for miracles" which produces so many unfounded stories and accounts for the presence of miraculous claims in all sorts of religions and cults?

The Bible offers some very clear answers on this topic. It denounces, on the one hand, an immoderate yearning for miracles. Jesus expressed a sort of fatigue on that score, because the people pressed around him to witness miracles. It was as if he felt harried and burdened by them. The Bible warns against the desire to "see miracles." Even on the day of the resurrection, for which it was necessary to have eyewitness testimony, Jesus says: "Blessed are those who have not seen and yet believe" (John 20:29 RSV). The Bible does not encourage "yearning for miracles." It must however be recognized, with all due humility, that we believers are of the same nature as all other men, the seed of regeneration in us does not change our impulses! The laws of collective psychology function just as well for us. It is thus quite true that, in evangelical circles, stories of miracles are concocted which seem highly doubtful. We are called to exercise in this respect a true critical sense. The Bible, for its part, exhorts us to soberness. This is evidenced in the stark contrast between the canonical Gospels and the apocryphal gospels, borne of popular expectations in the second century after Christ, with their gratuitous miracles, included simply for sensational effect. Even the Koran attributes such miracles to Jesus, who, at age two, would have come to the defense of his mother who had been accused of adultery.

The Bible emphasizes that false teachers, which is to say purveyors of false doctrine, will work miracles. It is not at all surprising, in this light, that miracles exist in all religions. False prophets and false Christs will come with miracles "so as to lead astray, if possible, even the elect" (Matthew 24:24 RSV). If we were left to ourselves, we would fall into the same trap as well, so strong in our hearts is this unhealthy craving, but God protects his elect! The Old Testament, likewise, solemnly warned long ago that if one tried to turn the people of God toward idols, even if he did great signs and wonders, he should be shown no quarter and must be completely shunned (Deuteronomy 13). The Bible envisions that wonders, through the power of Satan, may very well be wrought, as outside causalities which overrule the framework of cause and effect. Since the forces of evil are very much real, they can produce real effects. It is not surprising then that miracles occur in all religions. Other phenomena might be linked to laws of which we are not yet cognizant, such as psychosomatic healings through emotional release of the collective psyche.

The Bible warns believers not to allow themselves to fall into deception. Miracles are given as confirmatory signs of the message. When the Lord does bestow them, they must not be dismissed out of hand either, as if we were wiser or more correct in our understanding than God! The gospel was confirmed by miracles (Hebrews 2:2–4), so they indeed have a positive role. But it must first be the

Word itself, in the continuity of revelation, which is determinative. If there is no continuity of revelation, nor harmony with the teachings of the prophets of old, then the miracles are worthless and must instead be denounced as so many snares, as poisonous lures.

Miracles Unworthy of a God of Order?

Lastly, how shall we respond to the objection of those who think that miracles are unworthy of a God who has envisioned and established laws?

We might draw a preliminary response from C. S. Lewis's book on miracles. His response is nothing less than magisterial. He completely rejects the notion that miracles are a sort of divine improvisation to compensate for some deficiency. He thinks it better to compare miracles to poetry, to a skip in rhythm, to the irregularity which crowns a lyric work and makes it sublime. In the work of art, pure regularity never attains perfection. It is best not be "too" wise, as Ecclesiastes says. The *je ne sais quoi* which fills us with wonder is not found within regularity's precincts. Rather, the highest form of art introduces an irregularity so perfect in its right place that it delights our senses. We cannot imagine anything better. We would not want to change a single brushstroke, a single syllable. This is how the message of a poem jumps out to us in such a captivating way. And so it is that we must understand miracles. They are not so much a disruption of rhythm as a refinement of rhythm.

The second response is more theological. The interconnection of regular laws on the one hand and of extraordinary providences on the other corresponds exactly to the biblical relationship between God and the world. God is a rational and sovereign God, who can establish a universal order. If God were not sovereign, there would be no universal order. If he were not a rational God, there would be chaos. But at the same time, he superintends the world, he is a personal God. He is not simply the "cosmic reason" or the "system." He maintains his freedom, because he is above the world. That is precisely what stands out to us in his extraordinary providences. God, in this way, proposes a sign to those who have eyes to see. He reveals himself in his distinction from the world. He is present in the world, he sustains it, yet he does not reduce himself to its level, nor is he to be confused with it. That is what allows miracles to speak to us. The biblical God is the only being who can do miracles. A God who is not sovereign could not do them. Either it would be chaos or there would be laws that he could not overrule as he does. A God who is confused with the world would only in fact be the world under another name. We can thus honor the biblical teaching concerning miracles by seeing that it has a perfect correspondence, a full harmony with the biblical relationship between God and the world.

Conclusion

A comparison of the positions that account for the results, more or less definitive or provisional, of research in the domain of natural sciences (in particular in the field of origins) and for the findings in the domain of biblical interpretation does not reveal there to be any insurmountable conflict. This comparison confirms what might have been augured from the historical role of the Christian worldview as the breeding ground, nay the template for modern science. From the point of view of faith, the non-conflict (let us carefully choose our terms!) suggests that the scientific approach based on reason is *sound*, provided that it does not slip into reductionism and the illusion of pure independence. From the point of view of the scientific discipline, it shows that faith, in any case biblical faith, has nothing to do with gullibility. As a responsible commitment, faith has a passion for reality, which it honors and seeks to know in truth.

CONCLUSION

For whoever would save his life will lose it, but whoever loses his life for my sake will find it (Matthew 16:25 ESV). Jesus, the Master, employs a paradox to capture attention and to drive home a teaching. He does not engage in simple wordplay or play mind games. This is evidenced by the clause that interrupts the symmetry of his utterance: *for my sake.*

The truth that Jesus expresses then entails great existential consequences. He who preens in his presumption, with his will to power, or who clings to false hopes, seeking to save himself, actually cuts himself off from God and from others. His end is destruction. But he who pulls himself away from this deceptive dream and discerns in Christ the Way, the Truth, the Life, he who dares the wager of faith, a profitable wager for all eternity, finds true life.

This truth also holds in the domain of knowledge, the high calling of human nature. He who attributes to himself sovereign reason, the be all and end all, autonomous in the literal sense of the word (it is in itself its own law), is in the process of losing his mind. The waves of irrationalism which disorder our culture and wreak havoc in philosophy of science give ample evidence to that effect. He who is willing to lose his pseudosovereignty so that he might *think through faith*, that is, through the light of Christ Jesus as revealed in Scripture, that person will experience the fulfilment of a reason that renews itself, that opens itself, and that recreates itself with the Wisdom of God in the reality which he cherishes (see Proverbs 8:31). He who "loses" his old worldly reason *for the sake of Christ*, finds it again, redeemed, and quickened for eternity.

FOR FURTHER READING

A SHORT SELECT BIBLIOGRAPHY

The great classics are irreplaceable, beginning with Saint Augustine (*The Confessions*) and inevitably including the incomparable insight and appealing power of Pascal, whose *Pensées* are a must read (preferably in an edition in which the "fragment" numbering is standardized, such as Brunschvicg's or Lafuma's). Somewhat akin to an encyclopedic dictionary, *La Foi chrétienne et les défis du monde contemporain* (ed. Christophe Paya & Nicolas Farelly [Charols: Excelsis, 2013]) stands out as a useful resource.

In addition, the reader will find material to stimulate and nurture broader reflection in the following works:

Benton, John. *Cherche réponse*. Mulhouse: Grâce et Vérité, 1987.

Benz, Roland et al. *Des questions à vos réponses*. Lausanne: Presses Bibliques Universitaires, 1990. (Against overhasty or facile answers.)

Bluche, François. *Pourquoi croyez-vous en Dieu?* Paris: Criterion, 1994. (Testimonies from diverse personages, including myself.)

Translator's note: Blocher's bibliography is obviously geared toward a French-speaking audience. It is included here for those readers interested in learning about other French apologetic literature. Blocher also references several authors well known to the evangelical community of the English-speaking world. Their works are cited here in their original versions. The comments on each work are Blocher's.

Brun, Jean. *Philosophie et christianisme*. Québec/Lausanne: Édition du Beffroi/l'Âge d'homme, 1988. (The complete works of the philosopher, brilliant and sometimes difficult, in the tradition of Pascal and Kierkegaard, and having at least an indirect apologetic dimension.)

Chaunu, Pierre. *Le Chemin des mages. Entretiens avec Gérard Kuntz*. Lausanne: Presses Bibliques Universitaires, 1983. (No need to present the renowned historian.)

Clavier, Paul. *Dieu sans barbe. Vingt et une conversations instructives et amusantes sur la question très disputée de l'existence de Dieu*. Paris: La Table Ronde, 2002. (By a very serious Thomist, in spite of the title.)

Jaeger, Lydia. *Pour une philosophie chrétienne des sciences*. Collection: « Terre Nouvelle ». Cléon-d'Andran/Nogent-sur-Marne: Excelsis/Institut Biblique, 2000. (One of the worthwhile books by an author who has competencies in three fields: theology, physics, and philosphy.)

———. *Ce que les cieux racontent. La science* à *la lumière de la création*, Collection: « La Foi en dialogue ». Charols/Nogent-sur-Marne: Excelsis/Institut Biblique, 2008.

———. *L'Âme et le cerveau. L'enjeu des neurosciences*, Collection: « La Foi en dialogue ». Charols/Nogent-sur-Marne/Paris: Excelsis/Institut Biblique/Groupes Bibliques Universitaires, 2009. (Proceedings from a conference held at the Faculté Libre de Théologie Évangélique.)

———. *De la Genèse au génome. Perspectives bibliques et scientifiques sur l'évolution*, Collection: « La Foi en dialogue ». Charols/Nogent-sur-Marne/Paris: Excelsis/Institut Biblique/Groupes Bibliques Universitaires, 2011. (Proceedings from a conference of the Réseau des Scientitiques Évangéliques.)

———. *Adam, qui es-tu? Perspectives bibliques et scientifiques sur l'origine de l'humanité*, Collection: « La Foi en dialogue ». Charols/Paris: Excelsis/Groupes Bibliques Universitaires, 2013. (Proceedings from a conference of the Réseau des Scientitiques Évangéliques.)

Keller, Timothy. *The Reason for God: Belief in an Age of Skepticism.* New York: Dutton, 2008. (By an exceptionally effective pastor-thinker with a view to the youth of hipster culture.)

Lewis, C. S. *Mere Christianity.* New York: Macmillan, 1952. (Great synthesis of the work of the apologist par excellence.)

———. *God in the Dock.* Grand Rapids: Eerdmans, 1970.

———. *Miracles: A Preliminary Study.* Grand Rapids/New York: Macmillan, 1978.

McDowell, Josh. *The New Evidence That Demands a Verdict.* Nashville: Thomas Nelson, 1999.

McGrath, Alister. *Intellectuals Don't Need God & Other Modern Myths: Building Bridges to Faith through Apologetics.* Grand Rapids: Zondervan, 1993. (By an Anglican Evangelical Theologian who is both multitalented and prolific.)

Perron, Raymond. *Plaidoyer pour la foi chrétienne. L'apologétique de Cornelius Van Til.* Montréal: Faculté de Théologie Évangélique, 1996. (One of the first voices on the theology of the apologetic enterprise.)

Rhoton, Dale. *La Logique et la foi.* Braine-l'Alleud: Éditeurs de Littérature Biblique, 1967. (Pioneering work in French.)

Schaeffer, Francis A. *He Is There and He Is Not Silent.* Wheaton, IL: Tyndale House Publishers, 1972. (Along with Lewis, the other great apologist of the twentieth century.)

———. *The God Who Is There.* 30th anniversary ed. Downers Grove, IL: InterVarsity Press, 1998.

Schmitt, Yann. *Qu'est-ce qu'un Dieu?,* Collection « Chemins philosophiques ». Paris: J. Vrin, 2013. (By a French university philosopher.)

About the Author

Henri A. G. Blocher is an evangelical theologian who served at various institutions of higher learning in France from 1965–2003, before joining the faculty at Wheaton Graduate School from 2003–2008. He is currently Professor Emeritus of Systematic Theology at the Faculté Libre de Théologie Évangélique de Vaux-sur-Seine. Blocher earned a B.D. degree from Gordon Divinity School (now Gordon-Conwell Theological Seminary) in 1959, and earned his first doctorate in France in 1974. His second doctorate from Gordon-Conwell Theological Seminary followed in 1989. Dr. Blocher was awarded an honorary doctorate from Westminster Theological Seminary in 2014. He has written many books and articles in his native French, and taught in Africa, Australia, Canada, Europe, and the United States.

About the Translator

Damon DiMauro teaches French and Italian at Gordon College in Wenham, Massachusetts.